ANOTHER AMERICA

Also by Barbara Kingsolver

High Tide in Tucson
Pigs in Heaven
Animal Dreams
The Bean Trees
Homeland and Other Stories
Holding the Line: Women in the Great Arizona Mine Strike of 1983

BARBARA KINGSOLVER

ANOTHER AMERICA

OTRA AMERICA

CON TRADUCCIÓN ESPAÑOL
POR REBECA CARTES

SEAL PRESS

Cover design by Patrick David Barber
Cover photograph by Margaret Randall
Author photograph by Guy Mendes
Book design by Clare Conrad
Text composition by Patrick David Barber

Library of Congress Cataloging-in-Publication-Data
Kingsolver, Barbara.
    Another America = Otra América / con traducción Español por Rebeca Cartes. — 2nd ed.
    Bilingual text with poems in English and Spanish on facing p.
    ISBN 1-58005-004-2 (pbk.)
    1. Protest poetry, American—Translations into Spanish. 2. America—Social conditions—Poetry.
    3. Protest poetry, American. 4. Women—America—Poetry. 5. Poor—America—Poetry.
I. Cartes, Rebeca. II. Title.
PS3561. I496A87   1998
811'.54—dc21
                                             98-11519
                                                  CIP

Printed in the United States of America
Second edition, first printing April 1998

10   9   8   7   6   5   4   3   2

Distributed to the trade by Publishers Group West
In Canada: Publishers Group West, Toronto, Ontario
In Great Britain and Europe: Airlift Book Company, Middlesex, England
In Australia: Banyan Tree Book Distributors, Kent Town, South Australia

The following poems previously appeared in these publications:
"Deadline" appeared in *The American Voice* and in *Peace Prayers* (HarperSanFrancisco, 1991); "The Middle Daughter" and "Your Mother's Eyes" in *Calyx*; "This House I Cannot Leave" in *Clarion*; "Our Father Who Drowns the Birds" in *Heresies*; "Reveille" in *Kauri*; "The Loss of my Arms and Legs" and "For Richard After All" in the *Kentucky Poetry Review*; "Apotheosis" in the *New Mexico Humanities Review*; "Orang-Outang" in *Prickly Pear Poets*; "On the Morning I Discovered my Phone was Tapped" in *Sojourner*; "Remember the Moon Survives" in *Calyx* and in *The Courage to Heal* (HarperCollins, 1988); "Ten Forty-Four" in *Rebirth of Power* (Mother Courage Press, 1987).

Grateful acknowledgement is made for the use of excerpts from the following copyrighted material: Lyrics from "(Nothing But) Flowers" by David Byrne. Copyright © 1988 by Index Music Inc. (ASCAP); reprinted by permission of Warner Brothers. "Ourselves or Nothing" by Carolyn Forché Originally appeared in *The Country Between Us* (HarperCollins Publishers, New York, 1981). Copyright © 1981 by Carolyn Forché; reprinted by permission of HarperCollins Publishers. "I Am" by Angelo Logan. Originally appeared in *We Are Twilight When Bright Lights Start To Fall: Poetry from Galileo High School* (self-published). Copyright © 1990 by Angelo Logan; reprinted by permission. "The Eye" by Sharon Olds. Originally appeared in *The Dead and the Living* (Alfred A. Knopf, New York, 1984). Copyright © 1984 by Sharon Olds; reprinted by permission of Alfred A. Knopf. The lines from "Storm Warnings" from *The Fact of a Doorframe, Poems Selected and New, 1950-1984*, by Adrienne Rich, are used with the permission of the author and the publisher, W.W. Norton & Company, Inc. Copyright © 1984 by Adrienne Rich. Copyright © 1975, 1978 by W.W. Norton & Company, Inc. Copyright © 1981 by Adrienne Rich.

CONTENTS

FOREWORD by Margaret Randall   xi

INTRODUCTION   xv

I

THE HOUSE DIVIDED / LA CASA DIVIDIDA

Beating Time   3

Deadline   5

What the Janitor Heard in the Elevator   7

Reveille   9

Street Scenes   11

Waiting for the Invasion   15

Justicia   17

II

THE VISITORS / LOS VISITANTES

Refuge   21

For Sacco and Vanzetti   23

The Monster's Belly   27

In Exile   29

Escape   31

III

THE LOST / LOS PERDIDOS

American Biographies   35

This House I Cannot Leave   37

Ten Forty-Four   39

Portrait   43

Family Secrets   45

For Richard After All   49

The Loss of My Arms and Legs   51

IV

THE BELIEVERS / LOS CREYENTES

Bridges   59

Naming Myself   61

Apotheosis   63

Orang-Outang   65

Ordinary Miracle   67

Babyblues   69

Daily Bread   71

Watershed   73

Possession   75

Frankfort Cemetery   77

Poem for a Dead Neighbor   81

V

THE PATRIOTS / LOS PATRIOTAS

Our Father Who Drowns the Birds   87

On the Morning I Discovered My Phone Was Tapped   93

The Middle Daughter   97

In the City Ringed With Giants   99

The Blood Returns   103

Remember the Moon Survives   109

Your Mother's Eyes   115

ANOTHER AMERICA

FOREWORD

I AM READING Barbara Kingsolver's *Another America/Otra América*, again after several years. The poems affect me now as they did then: taking up permanent residence in my yearning memory, sometimes bringing tears, always sparking the simple joy that comes from recognition. Yes, once again these poems move me. But now I also have questions.

In these times of almost total cynicism, how does the committed poet bring a political poem to life? Once in our country it was considered merely unsophisticated or banal (strident some said, or blatant) to write of these things. To imagine that placing oneself square in the middle of the struggle for justice could be a position from which a poem could be made. Poets elsewhere understood that political commitment was as appropriate a place from which to write as any other. Here, most of us remained bound by the McCarthyite chill.

Then, inevitably, because we are all connected, because we are inheritors of César Vallejo and Violeta Parra as well as possessed by our own deepest passion and sensibilities, we began to emerge from that chill. Not unscathed, but conscious, angry, full-voiced. Adrienne Rich, Alice Walker, June Jordan and many others led the way. Mostly women. Mostly women of color. Again, it was acceptable to write about what they have done to us. And to others in our name. A great North American poetry exploded into life once more.

But then—I am speaking of the raging sixties, the seventies, almost to the end of the decade of the eighties—poetry of struggle had a receptive audience. Many of us had first-hand experience of people working collectively to change society. Others read the news. Against all manner of subtle and not so subtle silencing, the voices of change could be heard. And those voices echoed in our poems, reverberated, bounced back in a chorus of gratitude and solidarity that in turn energized those doing the hardest work. This reciprocity, too, became a part of our poetic process.

It is so much more difficult now. Since the collapse of what has been deemed "real socialism," since the loss of Nicaragua and the very mediated victories in El Salvador, Guatemala, parts of Africa and Asia, it is ever so much more challenging to keep faith with the quest for justice. Not to let go of the dream, admit to the failure, resign oneself to a world based in greed—too overwhelmingly powerful to change.

For once, back when we were young, some of us believed that poetry could change the world. We meant this literally as well as metaphorically. I am one who has not forgotten, who still believes, who knows without qualifying the statement that we will change this world—with our poems and with our lives. That we must change it, or there will be no world left to change.

And so, as a poet and as a reader of poetry, my questions now include some very basic ones: how, in the face of all that has been made "acceptable," can we successfully recreate the language? How may we empower our poems so they will go on changing lives? How can we write the voice that lives and sings in this time of devastating failure?

I am on a plane, returning from my most recent visit to Cuba. I open *Another America/Otra América* having just left that *otra* America now more other—yet more inspiring—than ever. I face re-entry, the return to my own America, so often "other" to me. And I read:

"I walked on water once. / It took more fear than faith and, truthfully, / the water was as safely locked beneath as I / was locked above." ("American Biographies," p. 35.) And "...I am thinking / of the man who broke and entered / me." ("This House I Cannot Leave," p. 37.) And "There is a season when all wars end: / when the rains come. / When the landscape opens its own eyes / and laughs at your talk of dying ...This is the season that renders / all things equal: the season of the arsonist-Creator. / When sun sets a fire in the clouds / that is indistinguishable from morning. / When *sunset* and *fire* and *morning* / are all the same word ... When *justice* is not a word / because it is air, and we breathe it." ("Our Father Who Drowns the Birds," pp. 87-89.)

I read these lines and I am renewed. I think of Adrienne Rich's masterful *What is Found There: Notebooks on Poetry and Politics*, especially where she quotes Trotsky's affirmation that "one cannot approach art as one can politics, not because artistic creation is a religious rite or something mystical ... but because it has its own laws of development, and above all because in artistic creation an enormous role is played by subconscious processes—slower, more idle and less subjected to management and guidance, just because they are subconscious." (New York: W. W. Norton & Company, 1993, p. 45.)

I understand, again, that poets like Barbara Kingsolver follow those laws of development, immerse themselves in the subconscious processes, offer us the dream: battered but intact. They are the keepers of the faith, particularly in times of grief.

We have used these poems and will use them again. We will keep them close to us, read them to ourselves and to our children, quietly and aloud, as anthems to a possible future as well as memories of a past that is not dead. We will read them in English and in Rebeca Cartes' Spanish—because these two languages linked give birth to a third.

And so I am more than ever grateful, in a time of terrible waiting and uncertain progress, for this new edition of Kingsolver's collection. In the poems I find beauty and power, and the answers to the questions that without these lines would be paralyzing indeed.

Margaret Randall
Albuquerque, New Mexico
December 1997

INTRODUCTION

I HAVE NEVER yet been able to say out loud that I am a poet.

It took me some thirty years and several published novels to begin calling myself a novelist, but finally now I can do that, I own up to it, and will say so in capital letters on any document requiring me to identify myself with an honest living. "Novelist," I'll write gleefully, chortling to think that the business of making up stories can be called an honest living, but there you are. It's how I keep shoes on my kids and a roof above us. I sit down at my desk every day and make novels happen: I design them, construct them, revise them, I tinker and bang away with the confidence of an experienced mechanic, knowing that patience and effort will get this troubled engine overhauled and this baby will hum.

Poetry is a different beast. I rarely think of poetry as something I make happen—it is more accurate to say that it happens to me. Like a summer storm, a house afire, or the coincidence of both on the same day. Like a car wreck, only with more illuminating results. I've overheard poems, virtually complete, in elevators or restaurants where I was minding my own business. (An occupational hazard: I think of eavesdropping as minding my business.) When a poem does arrive, I gasp as if an apple had fallen into my hand, and give thanks for the luck involved. They are everywhere, but easy to miss. I know I might very well stand under that tree all day, whistling, looking off to the side, waiting for a red delicious poem to fall so I could own it forever. But like as not, it wouldn't. Instead it will fall right while I'm in the middle of changing the baby, or breaking up a rodeo event involving my children and the dog, or wiping my teary eyes while I'm chopping onions and listening to the news; then that apple will land with a thud and roll under the bed with the dust bunnies and lie there forgotten and lost for all time. There are dusty, lost poems all over my house, I assure you. In yours too, I'd be willing to bet. Years ago I got some inkling of this when I attended a reading by one of my favorite poets,

Lucille Clifton. A student asked her about the brevity of her poems (thinking, I suspect, that the answer would involve terms like "literary retrenchment" and "parsimony"). Ms. Clifton replied simply that she had six children, and could only hold about twenty lines in memory until the end of the day. I felt such relief, that this great poet was bound by ordinary life, like me.

I've learned since then that most great poets are more like me, and more like you, than not. They raise children and chop onions, they suffer and rejoice, they feel blessed by any poem they can still remember at the end of the day. They may be more confident about tinkering with the engine, but they'll always allow that there's magic involved, and that the main thing is to pay attention. I have several friends who are poets of great renown, to whom I've confessed that creating a poem is a process I can't really understand or control. Every one of them, on hearing this, looked off to the side and whispered, "Me either!"

We're reluctant to claim ownership of the mystery. In addition, we live in a culture that doesn't put much stock in mystery. Elsewhere in the world, say in Poland or Nicaragua, people elect their poets to public office, or at the very least pay them a stipend to produce poetry, regularly and well, for the public good. (Poles and Nicaraguans evidently have their own ideas about the nature of an honest living.) Here we have no such class of person. Here, a poet may be prolific and magnificently skilled but even so it's not the poetry that's going to keep shoes on the kids and a roof overhead. I don't know of a single American poet who makes a living solely by writing poetry. I don't know why this is so. It makes me unspeakably sad, but it's true. Identifying your livelihood as "Poet" on an official form is the kind of thing that will make your bank's mortgage officer laugh very hard all the way into the manager's office, and back. So we're a timid lot, of necessity. We demur. At the most, we might confess, "I write poetry sometimes."

And so we do. Whether anyone pays us or respects us or calls us a poet or not, most of us feel a tickle behind our left ear when we catch ourselves saying, "You know, it was a little big, and really pretty ugly." We stop in our tracks when a child pointing to the sunset cries that the day is bleeding and is going to die. Poetry approaches, pauses, then skirts around us like a cat. I sense its presence in my house when I am chopping onions and crying but not really *crying* while I listen to the lilting radio newsman declare, "Up next: the city's oldest homeless shelter shut down by neighborhood protest, *and*, Thousands offer to adopt baby Jasmine abandoned in Disneyland!" There is some secret grief here I need to declare, and my fingers itch for a pencil. But then the advertisement blares that I should expect the unexpected, while my elder child announces that a shelter can't be homeless, but that onions make her eyes run away with her nose, and my youngest marches in a circle shouting Apple-Dapple! Come-Thumb-Drum! and poems roll under the furniture, left and right. I've lost so many I can't count them. I do understand, they fall when I'm least able to pay attention because poems fall not from a tree, really, but from the richly pollinated boughs of an ordinary life, buzzing as lives are, with clamor and glory. They are easy to miss but everywhere, poetry just *is*, whether we revere it or try to put it in prison. It is elementary grace, communicated from one soul to another. It reassures us of what we know and socks us in the gut with what we don't, it sings us awake, it's irresistible, it's congenital.

One afternoon lately, while my one-year-old stood on a chair reciting the poems she seems to have brought with her onto this planet, I heard on the news that our state board of education was dropping the poetry requirement from our schools. The secretary of education explained that it takes too much time to teach children poetry, when they are harder pressed than ever to master the essentials of the curriculum. He said that we have to take a good, hard look at what is essential, and what is superfluous.

"*Superfluous*," I said to the radio.

"Math path boo!" said my child, undaunted by her new outlaw status.

This one was not going to get away. I threw down my dishtowel, swept the baby off her podium, and carried her under my arm as we stalked off to find a pencil. In my opinion, when you find yourself laughing and crying both at once, that is the time to write a poem. Probably, it's the only honest living there is.

⌾

OVER THE YEARS I've forgotten enough poems to fill several books, and remembered enough to fill just one. This, so far, is it. By the grace of a small, devoted press and a small, devoted contingent of North Americans who read poetry, it has remained in print for five years now. I was happy when the publisher suggested printing a new edition that could include some more recent work, and delighted that my friend Rebeca Cartes could apply her remarkable skills to the translation of the new poems, maintaining the bilingual presentation of the original book. I was delighted again when my friend and mentor Margaret Randall, who was the first to read my poetry manuscript years ago and encourage me toward publication, agreed to write a foreword.

The work in this book spans many years. The opening poem of this new edition is the product of that recent afternoon when the board of education declared poetry obsolete. Another poem, "Portrait" (also new to this edition, but very old), I wrote in college, after seeking my first writing advice from an English professor, who advised: "Write sonnets. It will teach you discipline." I dutifully wrote a hundred dreadful sonnets and just this one that seemed successful, insofar as its subject suits the extremely confining sonnet form. The other new poems appear in this book's most joyful section, "The Believers," and reflect the main preoccupation of my recent life, the safe-keeping of children. But most of the work here was written in the decade or so after my arrival in Tucson at the very end of the 1970s.

I'd tried to write poetry all my life but—all those sonnets notwithstanding—I didn't really begin until my adulthood commenced, in Tucson, Arizona. I had come to the Southwest expecting cactus, wide open spaces, and adventure. I found, instead, another whole America. This was not picture postcards, or anything resembling what I had previously supposed to be American culture. Arizona was cactus all right, and purple mountains' majesty, but this desert that burned with raw beauty had a great fence built across it, attempting to divide north from south. I'd stumbled upon a borderland where people perished of heat by day and cold hostility by night.

This is where poetry and adulthood commenced for me, as I understand both those things, because of remarkable events that fell into my quite ordinary way. Oh, I suffered the extremes of love and loss, poverty and menial jobs and exhilarating recuperations, obsessive explorations of a new landscape, and these are all common things for a young adult in the America I knew. But I met people, some of them very uncommon. In particular, some of them were organizing the Sanctuary movement, something I could not previously have imagined in the America I knew. This was an underground railroad run by a few North Americans who placed conscience above law. Their risk was to provide safety to Latin American refugees—many hundreds of them—who faced death in their own countries, but were not legally admitted to ours. I learned, with horror, that the persecution these refugees fled was partly my responsibility. The dictators of El Salvador and Guatemala and Chile received hearty support from my government; their brutish armies were supplied and trained with the help of my taxes. My taxes also paid for the barbed wire and bullets that prevented war-weary families from finding refuge here. I wasn't prepared for the knowledge of what one nation will do to another. But knowledge arrived, regardless. I saw that every American proverb has two sides, can be told in two languages; that injustice does not disappear when you look away, but seeps in at the back of the neck to poison your soul. That unspeakable things can be survived, and sometimes there is joy on the other side. I learned all this, one story at a time, from people who had lived enough to know it. Some of them became my friends. Others disappeared again into places I can't know.

I believe there are wars in every part of every continent, and a world of clamor and glory in every life. This is mine. This is where I raise my voice and my children, and where we must find our peace if there is any to be had. Heartbreak and love and poetry abound. We live in a place where north meets south and many people are running for their lives, while many others rest easy with the embarrassments of privilege. Others, still, are trying to find a place in between, a place of honest living, where they can abide themselves and each other without howling in the darkness. My way of finding a place in this world is to write one. "Poet" is too much a title, I think, for something so incorrigible, and so I may never call myself by that name. But when I want to howl and cry and laugh all at once, I'll raise up a poem against the darkness. This is my testament to two Americas, and the places I've found, or made, or dreamed, in between.

Barbara Kingsolver
Tucson, Arizona
December 1997

I

THE HOUSE DIVIDED

LA CASA DIVIDIDA

These are the things that we have learned to do
Who live in troubled regions.

Adrienne Rich

If this is paradise
I wish I had a lawn mower.

David Byrne

LLEVANDO EL TIEMPO

conmemorando la eliminación de la poesía como requisito para las escuelas de Arizona, Agosto de 1997

El gobernador anuncia que la poesía ha sido expulsada
de nuestro currículum
dado que la metáfora y la rima le quitan tiempo
a la ciencia. La sapiencia de
nuestros niños se basa
en las cosas con que podemos llevar la cuenta. Las leyes
de la ingeniería. La poesía lleva tiempo, y el tiempo
es oro. Dijo: La suerte está echada.

La voz del gobernador cayó por el azogue
el microchip arrulló con su canción y la ley, ella fue
entregada a su audiencia. Los estudiantes
de ingeniería se inclinaron hacia sus números en clases
silenciosas, donde los ventiladores tentadores
susurraban "yo soy yo soy" en pentámetros yámbicos.
Los números indisciplinados y caprichosos fueron descartados
al sonar la campana.
En las arrugadas, desechadas ecuaciones,
pequeñas figuras negras en forma de renacuajos
formaron una nación, desapercibidas, en el papelero.

Afuera, una tormenta está a punto de agrietar el cielo.
Los rayos arañarán los secos cauces de los ríos, arrancando el barro
como un arado, bramando, llevándose puentes,
inesperadamente.
Los niños demasiado pequeños para saber
de la reciente muerte de la poesía
correrán a las ventanas para ver con qué pueden contar.
Danzarán a los yambos eléctricos de los ventiladores,
susurrando rimas ilícitas,
buscando una señal en el firmamento
mientras la lluvia lleva el tiempo.

BEATING TIME

commemorating the removal of poetry as a requirement in
Arizona's schools, August 1997

The Governor interdicted: poetry is evicted
from our curricula,
for metaphor and rhyme take time
from science. Our children's self-reliance rests
upon the things we count on. The laws
of engineering. Poeteering squanders time, and time
is money. He said: let the chips fall where they may.

The Governor's voice fell down through quicksilver
microchip song hummed along and the law
was delivered to its hearing. The students
of engineering bent to their numbers in silent
classrooms, where the fans overhead
whispered "I am I am" in iambic pentameter.
Unruly and fractious numbers were discarded at the bell.
In the crumpled, cast-off equations,
small black figures shaped like tadpoles
formed a nation, unobserved, in the wastepaper basket.

Outside, a storm is about to crack the sky.
Lightning will score dry riverbeds, peeling back the mud
like a plow, bellowing, taking out bridges,
completely unexpectedly.
The children too young to have heard
of poetry's demise turn their eyes
to the windows, to see what they can count on.
They will rise and dance to the iamb of the fans,
whispering illicit rhymes,
watching the sky for a sign
while the rain beats time.

PLAZO FIJO

15 de enero, 1991

La noche antes del comienzo de la guerra aún estás aquí.
Te quedas de pie en un frío y sofocado
océano de velas, mil versiones de tu misma cara
blanqueada desde abajo por la clara luz de cera.
Una vigilia. Te preguntas cuántas cosas
son dignas de esta fe.

Tienes una hija. Sus mejillas se curvan
en aspectos de la pera perfecta de Mohammed.
Tiene tres años. Demasiado niña para velas pero
tú estás aquí, es la guerra.
Las llamas codician el rubio destello de las puntas de su pelo,
su chaqueta de nylon riendo de color,
inflamable. Te has entregado entera
para traerla intacta hasta este momento,
y en el desierto, a esta hora, espera una bomba
que lanza gasolina en una sábana líquida,
un chasquido de ropa recién lavada sobre las cabezas,
       ancha como el Tigris antiguo,
inflamada en su descenso.

Las encuestas ya han cantado su ópera de aprobación: la tierra
desea guerra. Pero hay otra América,
la de gargantas de velas, segura como la marea.
Quienquiera que seas, también eres esta rabia de granito.
En la historia, tú serás los muertos vigilantes
que estuvieron de pie frente a cada guerra, con ancianos corazones
en tus bolsillos, de pie sobre el cadáver de la esperanza
para escuchar el trueno de sus plumas.

El desierto es hielo en diamante
       y solo estrellas sobre nuestras cabezas, aquí
y en todas partes, mil causas de una clara estrella de cera,
un holocausto de firmamento
y en algún lugar, un escape.

DEADLINE

January 15, 1991

The night before war begins, and you are still here.
You can stand in a breathless cold
ocean of candles, a thousand issues of your same face
rubbed white from below by clear waxed light.
A vigil. You are wondering what it is
you can hold a candle to.

You have a daughter. Her cheeks curve
like aspects of the Mohammed's perfect pear.
She is three. Too young for candles but
you are here, this is war.
Flames covet the gold-sparked ends of her hair,
her nylon parka laughing in color,
inflammable. It has taken your whole self
to bring her undamaged to this moment,
and waiting in the desert at this moment
is a bomb that flings gasoline in a liquid sheet,
a laundress's snap overhead, wide as the ancient Tigris,
and ignites as it descends.

The polls have sung their opera of assent: the land
wants war. But here is another America,
candle-throated, sure as tide.
Whoever you are, you are also this granite anger.
In history you will be the vigilant dead
who stood in front of every war with old hearts
in your pockets, stood on the carcass of hope
listening for the thunder of its feathers.

The desert is diamond ice and only stars above us here
and elsewhere, a thousand issues of a clear waxed star,
a holocaust of heaven
and somewhere, a way out.

LO QUE ESCUCHO EL CONSERJE
EN EL ELEVADOR

La mujer de las pulseras de oro le dice a su amiga:
tuve que despedir a otra más.
¿Te imaginas?
Quebró el jarrón que Jack me regaló
para Navidad.
Era uno de esos, tú sabes, que iba
con todo. Todos mis colores.
Le pregunté a él si no le importaría
que compre otro igual.
Era el único que siempre se veía bien.

Su amiga dice:
Búscate una que hable inglés.
Es una gran ventaja.

La mujer del oro está de acuerdo
en que sería una gran ventaja.

WHAT THE JANITOR HEARD
IN THE ELEVATOR

The woman in gold bracelets tells her friend:
I had to fire another one.
Can you believe it?
She broke the vase
Jack gave me for Christmas.
It was one of those,
you know? That worked
with everything. All my colors.
I asked him if he'd mind
if I bought one again just like it.
It was the only one that just always worked.

Her friend says:
Find another one that speaks English.
That's a plus.

The woman in gold agrees
that is a plus.

TOQUE DE DIANA

Soy la mujer cuya carne
no se mueve cuando camina,
la sin pezones,
la sin sangre, la mujer sin sudor
que llora lágrimas copiosas por la tensión
que le causan todas las otras secreciones prohibidas.
Estoy pintada con los colores de ninguna flor
que nunca floreció en realidad,
no huelo como ninguna otra cosa viviente.
Soy la mujer en guerra contra el vello del cuerpo:
la que encrespa su cabello oriental,
alisa su cabello africano,
la que adereza sus párpados con pelos
y los arranca de sus cejas,
los persigue y destruye implacablemente
declarando guerra a sus orígenes mamíferos.
Literalmente, me has visto más de un millón de veces:
la mujer completamente modificada que no se distingue
entre la muchedumbre
de mujeres completamente modificadas,
y yo perduro porque
el potencial de mi cuerpo es un universo.
Si abandonara esta batalla
y cambiara mi furia piadosa
por algo menos persistente y más conquistable que mi sexo,
si me fuera a la guerra
y dejara atrás mis campos sin segar,
sin maquillar, y permitiera que crecieran las hierbas,
si decidiera llegar a ser
el animal que soy, ¿entonces
qué?

REVEILLE

I am the woman whose flesh
does not move when she walks,
the nipple-less,
the bloodless, sweatless woman
who cries copious tears from the pressure
of all other prohibited secretions.
I am painted in the colors of no flower
that ever really bloomed,
I do not smell like any living thing.
I am the woman at war with body hair: who
curls her oriental hair,
straightens her African hair,
garnishes her eyelids with hair
and removes it from her eyebrows,
pursues it and relentlessly destroys it,
engaged in war with her mammalian origins.
Literally you have seen me a million times:
the radically altered female who doesn't stand out
in the crowd
of radically altered females,
I remain because
the potential of my body is a universe.
If I should abandon this battle
and turn my pious fury on something
less persistent, more conquerable than my sex,
if I should go away to war
and leave my fields behind, unmowed,
unmanicured, and let the weeds spring up,
if I were to become
the animal that I am, then
what?

ESCENAS CALLEJERAS

I.

El día en que mi hermana se fue para siempre,
vino a mi trabajo, su automóvil cargado,
a decirme adiós.
Tomadas de los brazos, un cerrojo
a punto de ser forzado, caminamos
a lo largo del estacionamiento, temerosas
y seguras desde la niñez
de que cada separación sería definitiva.
Desde la calle
nos observaban varios muchachos en un automóvil.
En el momento en que la solté
gritaron,
¡mariconas!

II.

Los tres estaban sentados fumando
sobre una pared frente a la escuela:
él en medio, ella
a su derecha, a su izquierda,
ninguno de ellos mayor de quince.
El dijo, cuando pasé,

STREET SCENES

I.

The day my sister moved away forever,
she came by where I work, her car
packed, to tell me goodbye.
With arms linked, a lock
about to be forced, we walked
the parking lot, afraid
and sure since childhood
that every separation would be final.
A carload of young men watched
from the street.
At the moment I let her go
they yelled, *Hey,*
dykes.

II.

The three of them sat smoking
on a wall in front of the high school:
he in the middle, she
on his right, on his left,
not one of them older than fifteen.
He said, as I walked past,

no me vendría mal un
pedazo de eso.
Me sorprendió en un mal día, giré sobre mis talones
y le enrostré un puño italiano.
La de su derecha, dijo, *hija' e puta.*

III.

Mi hermana y yo otra vez, en un pueblo fronterizo,
hartas de ser altas, blancas, de que nos siguieran,
cansadas y quizás temerosas de uno que
silbando, insistente,
nos siguió por media hora:
nos dimos vuelta de repente,
observamos sus manos en los bolsillos,
sus brazos, el vello del cuello,
nos miramos y reímos.
Cuchicheando como si tuviéramos un secreto
o un conocimiento superior, lo seguimos
hasta el otro lado de la plaza. Desde allí,
escapó a la carrera.

I could use
a piece of that.
A bad day for me, I spun on my heel,
showed him an Italian fist.
She, on his right, said *Bitch.*

III.

My sister and I again, in a border town,
fed up with being tall, fair, followed,
tired and maybe afraid of the one who,
hissing, persistent,
trailed us for half an hour:
we turned all at once,
examined the hands in his pockets,
the arms, the hair on his neck,
looked at each other and laughed.
Whispering the pretense of a secret, superior
knowledge, we followed him
down to the end of the plaza.
From there, he ran.

ESPERANDO LA INVASION

Otros años he observado el cielo buscando a los pájaros
que vuelan en formación hacia el Sur.
Este año pasan por mi sueño en líneas intactas
empujados sobre alas mecánicas.

Reconozco la voz que usas
para decir a tus niños que no teman
a cada zumbido
que dispersa sus juegos como granada de metralla
o hielo astillado resbalando en el asfalto;
cada proximidad
los lanza bajo los camiones
en un montón de extremidades, lanza a
los pequeños, que corren bajo tus pechos
que duelen como la cabra sin ordeñar cuyos balidos se oyen a lo lejos,
que duelen por la espera.

Cada niño ha esperado a ángeles de muerte: yo escuchaba
en la noche, esperando a los rusos, que
reconocerían nuestro pueblito
por sus torres de agua gemelas.
Créanme, alguien pintó las torres de negro
con la esperanza de salvarnos.
Y aún ahora el miedo es un animal nocturno,
máquinas que pulsan sus alas y el susurro
de mi madre rezando
en la cama donde nunca murió.

Nadie se deslizó por un lago de cielo nocturno
en busca de nuestras torres secretas.
Nadie. Eso lo entiendo ahora, pero algunos creyeron
y creyendo aún, preparan la masacre.

WAITING FOR THE INVASION

In other years I watched the sky for birds
flying south in formation.
This year they pass in unbroken lines through my sleep,
driven down on machine wings.

I know the voice you use
for telling children not to fear
every droning sound
that scatters their play like shrapnel or shattered
ice across asphalt; every approach sends them
into piles of limbs under trucks,
sends the youngest under your breasts
that ache like the unmilked she-goat bleating somewhere,
ache with the waiting.

Every child has waited for death angels: I
listened at night for the Russians, who would
know our little town
by its twin water towers.
Someone, believe this, painted the towers black
hoping to save us.
And even now, fear is a night-time animal,
winged engines pulsing and the drone
of my mother praying
in the bed where she never died.

No one slipped through a lake of night sky
in search of our secret towers.
No one. I know this now, but some believed
and believing still, prepare the massacre.

JUSTICIA

Los encantamientos salvajes de nuestros sueños
traen, por la puerta,
al lobo.
En su ojo de carbón,
el sol austral es pedernal.
La imagen de una persona, pequeña y perfecta, brilla
en el espejo de su córnea.
Su dolor anaranjado se vuelve atardecer del desierto.
Su hambre percibe esencia de sangre en el viento,
el sueño de animales en sus refugios,
todo menos fronteras.
La televisión dice que McAllen, Texas
está más cerca de Managua que de Washington, D. C.
y las amas de casa en McAllen
revisan sus propios
posibles ojos bolcheviques en el espejo
y aseguran las ventanas.
Su constitución de paz canta de libertad y justicia
y sus sueños proscritos
dicen que el lobo merece un banquete.

JUSTICIA

The feral incantations of our dreams
bring the wolf
through the door.
The southern sun is flint
on his charcoal eye.
The image of a person, tiny and perfect, shines
in the mirror of his cornea.
His orange pain becomes a desert sunset.
His hunger perceives the scent of blood
on the wind,
the sleep of sheltered animals,
everything
but borders.
The television says McAllen, Texas,
is closer to Managua than to Washington, D.C.,
and housewives in McAllen
check their own
possibly Bolshevik eyes in the mirror
and lock the windows.
Their peaceful constitution sings of liberty
and justice
and their outlaw dreams
say the wolf deserves a meal.

II

THE VISITORS

LOS VISITANTES

*America prepares with composure and good will
for the visitors that have sent word.*

Walt Whitman

REFUGIO

a Juana, violada por oficiales de inmigración y deportada

Tiéndeme tu mano,
te dirá. *Alcánzame*
atravesando siglos de alambres de púas
y desierto. Aprovecha lo último
de tu hambre
para llegar a mí. Yo
tomaré tu mano.
La tomo.

Primero
él la desdoblará
desde la palma hacia los dedos
para observarla
y ver que no ofrece nada.

Para entonces,
con una hoja afilada,
cortarla.

Lanza el resto de ti
al mar de tus
hermanos de sangre.
Pero se queda con tu mano,
limpia,
protegida en una vitrina
iluminada:
        Evidencia,
te dirá,
de lo apetecible
que resulta
mi país.

REFUGE

for Juana, raped by immigration officers and deported

Give me your hand,
he will tell you. *Reach*
across seasons of barbed wire
and desert. Use the last
of your hunger
to reach me. I will
take your hand.
Take it.

First
he will spread it
fingers from palm
to look inside,
see it offers nothing.

Then
with a sharp blade
sever it.

The rest he throws back
to the sea of your
blood brothers.
But he will keep your hand,
clean, preserved in a glass case
under lights:
                Proof
he will say
of the great
desirability
of my country.

A SACCO Y VANZETTI

"Todos los que conocen estos dos brazos saben bien que no necesito matar a un hombre para robar su dinero. Puedo vivir con mis dos brazos, y vivir bien . . . En toda mi vida nunca robé y nunca maté. He luchado, desde que tengo uso de razón, para eliminar estos crímenes de la tierra."

de la última declaración de Bartolomeo Vanzetti al jurado, Nueva York, 1927

Por lo que conozco de cuero de zapatos y pescados,
a lo mejor dos hombres que tenían mucha hambre de pan
se pronunciarían para que se rechace un festín, y la esencia
ardiente de la sed del mediodía
buscaría y encontraría la mesa
donde los vasos de cristal fluyen
de vinagre y sal.

Por lo que conozco, el barco elegiría la niebla
y nunca querría la sirena del puerto
que anuncia, por entre la bruma
del deshonor de un hombre agonizante,
su canción única:
borrar estos crímenes de la tierra.

Pero ¿qué puedo hacer con este mar
en la cuencas de mis ojos? no por
la pérdida de dos buenos brazos, por Sacco, por Vanzetti,
si solo hubiera bastante mar; ni por los Rosenberg,
Ethel, sus dos hijos desgarrados
como nudos de la tela, entre alaridos.

Hemos estado muriendo durante todas nuestras vidas.
Mis lágrimas se derraman solo por la mañana, que
        ha llegado otra vez
a una ribera de huesos golpeados, y debo apretar en mis brazos
este día

FOR SACCO AND VANZETTI

"Everyone who knows these two arms knows well that I did not need to kill a man and take money. I can live with my two arms, and live well . . . In all my life I never stole and never killed. I have struggled, since I began to reason, to eliminate these crimes from the earth."

Bartolomeo Vanzetti's statement to the jury, New York, 1927

For all I know of shoeleather and fish,
maybe two men who hungered for bread would speak
to turn away a feast, and the heated core
of noonday thirst would seek and find the table
where crystal glasses are poured
with vinegar and salt.

For all I know the ship would choose the fog
and never want for the harbor bell
that peals, through the thickness
of a dying man's dishonor, its only song:
to erase these crimes from the earth.

But what can I do with this ocean
in the sockets of my eyes? Not for
the loss of two good arms, for Sacco, for Vanzetti,
if there were only sea enough; nor the Rosenbergs,
Ethel, her two babies torn
like knots from the cloth, screaming.

We have been dying all our lives.
My tears are just for morning, washed up again
on a shore of pounded bones, and I must hold this day

como una madre aprieta en sus brazos a su hijo de ojos oscuros
y se derrama como un río,
enseñándole a valerse con sus propias manos,

mis lágrimas se derraman porque debo amar este día
como el aire sudoroso del taller se inclina hacia
el perfume precioso del cuero,
como el pescado que ha quedado sobre el césped
con los ojos desmesurados
muerde el aire vacío y ama
su sueño de musgo húmedo,

como un hombre que va a morir ama las cosas que tocó
con sus dos buenas manos, aunque a la caída de la noche
esas manos serán dos nudos inertes
desgarrados de las ropas.
Este es el precio que exigen
los agonizantes que aman sus vidas.

Nicola Sacco y Bartolomeo Vanzetti, un zapatero y un vendedor de pescado, eran inmigrantes italianos que fueron ejecutados en 1927. Durante el juicio se les cuestionó acerca de sus actividades como organizadores obreros y anti bélicos, aunque habían sido acusados de un robo y un crimen que otros dos hombres más tarde confesaron haber cometido.

as a mother holds her dark-eyed infant son
and empties herself like a river,
teaches him life by his hands,

my tears are because I have to love this day
as the sweated air of the shop leans toward
the precious scent of leather,
as the fish thrown up wide-eyed on grass
bites on empty air and loves
its dream of watery moss,

as a dying man loves the things he touched
with his good hands, though by nightfall
they will be limp knots
torn from the cloth.
This is the price exacted from
the dying who love their lives.

Nicola Sacco and Bartolomeo Vanzetti, a shoemaker and a fish peddler, were Italian immigrants executed in 1927. At trial they were questioned mainly about their labor organizing and anti-war activities, though ostensibly charged with a robbery and murder to which two other men eventually confessed.

LAS ENTRAÑAS DEL MONSTRUO

a Ernesto Cardenal

Durante la aridez épica de mis años de infancia,
aprendí a lanzarme bajo mi escritorio
para sobrevivir a la lluvia de bombas cubanas.
Aprendí a arrodillarme sobre el suelo astillado
y con el fervor carnal
de un cuerpo adolorido de aburrimiento y rodillas torturadas,
rezar a Dios para que los comunistas
no vinieran y nos obligaran a dejar de rezar.

Y ahora, Padre Ernesto, descubro que habías
estado allí todo el tiempo,
con los monjes de Getsemaní, Kentucky.
Podría haber caminado hasta allí
en mis zapatos rudos, podría haberte visitado a ti
y a tu Señor risueño que hizo caer la mejor lluvia
sobre frijoles y arroz. Qué diferencia
haber conocido a este Señor, o saber por lo menos
que compartíamos el mismo pedacito de cielo, el que prometió
que un monstruo de cuernos y cabezas
saldría del mar
con el propósito de destruir la tierra.
En tu camisa oscura olorosa a hojas,
habría vaciado el dolor de mi niñez natural
para encontrar un amor más grande que el fin del mundo.

Pero los caminos que conocía se perdieron al final del pueblo
en bosques de sauces y aprensión. Tú y yo
no estábamos más cerca que lo que están los vivos y los muertos
que comparten un cementerio un domingo por la tarde.
Padre Ernesto, tú eras un ciudadano del dominio
de tu profundo deseo de destruir al monstruo,
y yo estaba ya en sus entrañas.

THE MONSTER'S BELLY

to Ernesto Cardenal

In the epic drought of my growing years,
I practiced leaping under my desk
to survive the rain of Cuban bombs.
I learned to kneel on a splintered floor
and with the carnal fervor
of a body aching from boredom and tortured knees,
to pray to God that the Communists
wouldn't come, and make us stop praying.

Now, Father Ernesto, I find you were there all along
with the monks at Gethsemani, Kentucky.
I could have walked there
in my blunt shoes, could have visited you
and your laughing Lord who made the best rain fall
on beans and rice. What a difference
to have known this Lord, or at least to know
he shared the same small sky with mine, who promised only
that the horned and headed monster
would come out of the sea
for the purpose of ending the world.
In your dark shirt smelling of leaves,
I would empty out the ache of my natural childhood
to find some greater love than the end of the world.

But the roads I knew were lost at the edge of town
in willow forests of apprehension. You and I
were no closer than the living and the dead
who share a cemetery on a Sunday afternoon.
Father Ernesto, you were a citizen of the domain
of your profound desire to kill the monster,
and I was already in its belly.

EN EXILIO

para Rebeca

Estas montañas que amo
son los nudillos
de un puño
que aplasta tus sueños contra la tierra.

Entre tanto, un fantasma-mujer sube a los autobuses de la ciudad
que conociste, eleva sus ojos hacia otro horizonte,
viviendo la vida que tú habías planeado.

Miles de vidas como ésta se mueven
por Santiago, invisibles como una década sin días.
Sus colores se desangraron a través de
las últimas puertas abiertas de Chile
mientras Víctor Jara acurrucó su alma en su puño
y la lanzó a una estrella fría
y Allende dejó de vivir.

En las calles cerca de tu hogar
un fantasma-mujer se desliza
a través de muros que aún no se construyeron,
a través de árboles que han crecido sorprendentemente
en catorce años.

Conocerte
es aprender a resistir la belleza
de la única rosa escarlata en un vaso.
Pareciera que pertenece a mi mesa
si no fuera por raíces y hojas,
la posibilidad de fruto,
el tallo
que sólo es cortado una vez.

IN EXILE

for Rebeca

These mountains I love
are knuckles
of a fist
that holds your dreams to the ground

while a ghost-woman boards the city buses
you knew, lifts her eyes to another horizon,
living the life you planned.

A thousand lives like hers move
through Santiago, invisible as a decade without days.
Their colors bled out through the last
open doors of Chile
while Victor Jara curled his soul in his fist
and threw it to a cold star
and Allende died.

In the streets near your home
a ghost-woman moves
through walls that were not yet built,
through trees that have grown surprisingly
in fourteen years.

To know you
is to learn to resist the beauty
of the single red rose in a glass.
It could belong on my table
were it not for roots and leaves,
the possibility of fruit,
the stem
that is only cut once.

EXPIACION

En Palestina, en los días
anteriores a todo excepto Dios,
los creyentes prepararon dos cabritos.
Uno fue sacrificado.
Al segundo se le permitió escapar
como por casualidad, a las montañas:
el chivo expiatorio
con los pecados del mundo sobre su lomo.

Puedo caminar tus calles fingiendo
un destino exacto.
Pero nuestros ojos nunca se cruzan. Tú me conoces.
He escapado de mi patria, esperanzada
como un lagarto que quiere quedar limpio
        después de un cambio de piel.

Mi nación tiene puertas anchas como graneros
para que acudan los creyentes
corriendo sobre pezuñas oscuras
a través de tus ciudades,
donde rojas cascadas de flores
suspiran por la conquista.
Nuestros pies repiquetean sobre tus piedras
pero no nos llevamos nada.
Los pecados
todavía están allí, manchando el altar.

ESCAPE

In Palestine, in the days
before anything but God,
the believers prepared two goats.
One was sacrificed.
The second was allowed to run away
as if by accident into the mountains:
the escape-goat,
with everyone's sins on its back.

I can move through your streets feigning
an exact destination
but our eyes never touch. You know me.
I have fled my homeland, hopeful
as a lizard pulling clean from an old skin.

My nation has doors as wide as granaries
to turn the believers out
to run here on dark hooves,
through your cities,
where red cascades of flowers
sigh of the conquest.
Our feet click on your stones
but we've carried off nothing.
The sins
are still back there, staining the altar.

III

THE LOST

LOS PERDIDOS

I am a person of few words.
I have seen things which nobody else should see
I was found but now I'm lost.

> Angelo Logan
> Galileo High School
> San Francisco, 1990

BIOGRAFIAS AMERICANAS

1.

Una vez caminé sobre el agua.
Me costó más miedo que fe, y verdaderamente,
el agua estaba tan segura bajo mis pies como yo
estaba segura sobre ella.

2.

Cuando el miedo llega sin palabras
acurrucada en la oscuridad de frazadas empujo una mano
hacia mi corazón para poder ser la primera
en saber que he muerto.

3.

En plenitud fingida podría caminar la larga
solitaria distancia entre todos los puntos y todos los otros
porque en su enlace mi geometría habrá
sido fiel a sus propias leyes imaginadas.

AMERICAN BIOGRAPHIES

1.

I walked on water once.
It took more fear than faith and, truthfully,
the water was as safely locked beneath as I
was locked above.

2.

When the fear comes wordless I
wombcurled in blanket darkness push one hand
into my heart so I will be the first
to know that I have died.

3.

In feigned completeness I would walk the lonely
longest distance between all points and all others
because in their connection my geometry will have
been faithful to its own imagined laws.

ESTA CASA QUE NO PUEDO DEJAR

Mi amiga describe al ladrón:
cómo tocó sus ropas, caminó por las habitaciones
dejando allí su persona,
                          manchando el espacio
entre las paredes, ella puede verlo.

No le importa qué se llevó, sólo
que la ha desalojado, no puede
quedarse en esta casa
que amó, los colores de cuatro familias raspados
de las paredes para pintar los suyos,
para plantar lo suyo.
Dejará abandonados los árboles frutales.

Venderá, se irá, quizás
otro vecindario.
                  La gente dice
olvídalo. El mercado no está bueno. Le aconsejan
que piense en vender la hipoteca,
que piense en los árboles frutales

pero los árboles han dejado de crecer para ella.

No le aconsejo nada.
Le digo que sé, que se irá. Pienso
en el hombre que entró por la fuerza

en mí.

        De los años que me costó estar otra vez
en esta casa que no puedo dejar.

THIS HOUSE I CANNOT LEAVE

My friend describes the burglar:
how he touched her clothes, passed through rooms
leaving himself there,
                              staining the space
between walls, a thing she can see.

She doesn't care what he took, only
that he has driven her out, she can't
stay in this house
she loved, scraped the colors of four families
from the walls and painted with her own,
and planted things.
She is leaving fruit trees behind.

She will sell, get out, maybe
another neighborhood.
                              People say
Get over it. The market isn't good. They advise
that she think about cash to mortgage
and the fruit trees

but the trees have stopped growing for her.

I offer no advice.
I tell her I know, she will leave. I am thinking
of the man who broke and entered

me.

    Of the years it took to be home again
in this house I cannot leave.

DIEZ CUARENTA Y CUATRO

Esto es lo que pasó.
En el calor de polen de un Agosto,
uno de esos días cuando el sol
llena tu piel como una hoja,
yo estaba en mi patio,
visitando los árboles.
De pronto,
un hombre de limpia camisa azul
estaba allí,
esperando a que lo viera,
esperando como si para siempre.
Muy amable, tenía un problema,
dijo que su automóvil estaba descompuesto.
Su boca era una caverna pálida.
Necesitaba entrar, librarse del sol.
Me preguntó si podía
pedirme un favor.
En aquellos días yo tenía el hábito
de decir que sí,
aún antes de preguntar
¿qué desea?
Me siguió a la casa.
Le serví agua en un vaso de loza china,
china, una corona de rosas antiguas,
y luego él preguntó
si podría hacer una cosa más.
Sentí, antes de ver,
la punta inoxidable entre mis costillas
dirigida hacia mi latido,
un tesoro en una jaula
que se abre fácilmente.
La cerradura no fue ningún problema.
Dije, "sí, lo haré."
No pregunté, "¿qué es lo que desea?"

TEN FORTY-FOUR

This is all that happened.
In the pollen heat of an August,
one of those days when the sun
fills your skin like a leaf,
I was in my yard,
visiting the trees.
A man in a clean blue shirt
stood waiting, suddenly,
for me to notice,
waiting as if forever.
Polite enough, in trouble,
said his car broke down.
His mouth was a pale cave.
He needed to get in out of the sun.
He asked if he could
ask me for a favor.
In those days it was my habit
to say I would,
even before I asked
what do you want?
He followed me in.
I poured water in a china cup,
china, a wreath of antique roses,
and then he asked
if I would do just one more thing.
I felt, before I saw
the stainless point between my ribs
dead center on the heartbeat,
a treasure in a cage
so easily opened.
Nothing at all to the lock.
I said, "Yes I will."
I didn't ask, "What is it

Fue la última vez.
Ese era mi cuchillo, lo había usado
cientos de días para pelar
mis vegetales, y el lo usó
conmigo con la misma idea, pelando de mí lo que había
de fe.

Los oficiales vinieron pronto
como si hubieran estado esperando.
Tomaron huellas digitales de todo incluyéndome a mí
y comunicaron sin tregua por sus radios
que había ocurrido un diez cuarenta y cuatro en la calle 8.
Así lo llamaron.
Esos hombres que llevan pistolas
no podían llamar por su nombre
lo que me había sucedido. En cambio
recolectaron huellas
de mi cuerpo,
del vaso quebrado, cosas
que no podrían haber estado más vacías.
Una huella de cabello o sangre o semen
para capturarlo.
Un olor
para la caza.

Nunca lo encontraron. Y extrañamente,
no espero que vuelva,
aquí ya no hay nada para él. Ni plata
bajo la cama,
ni confianza.
Lo guardo en un cajón con llave con mis cuchillos de cocina
y otras cosas mías que han sido usadas contra mí.

that you want?"
It was the last time.
That knife was mine, I'd used it
on a hundred days to peel
my vegetables, and with that exact
regard for me he used it, peeled off what there was
of faith.

The officers came promptly
as if they had been waiting.
Fingerprinted everything including me
and stated endlessly into their open radios
that there had been a ten forty-four on 8th street.
That's what they called it.
These men who carry guns
couldn't bring themselves to call by name
what had been done to me. Instead
they gathered traces
from my body,
from the broken cup, things
that could not have been more empty.
A trace of hair or blood or sperm
to bring him down.
A scent
for the hunt.

They didn't
ever find him. And
I don't expect him back,
he's finished here. No silver
under the bed,
no trust.
I keep it in a locked drawer with my kitchen knives
and other things of mine that have been used against me.

RETRATO

La dama como puede ha protestado
y a su disposición cuenta con ellos,
los ofrendados medios: pasión, vuelo
al alcance de una orden frustrado;
alas de ópalo, cuya fineza
con sus alas de mosca al cielo abraza.
Un corazón sí tiene, más su gracia
de construcción cristalina, no muestra
corazón en su interior, o que pueda
contener lo que contiene. En jaula
de oropel, su locura fino habla;
su rabia abortada sangra lenta,
dolor pastel; cautívales, lloroso,
el exquisito verdor de sus ojos.

PORTRAIT

The lady doth protest as best she can
and has at her disposal those, the right
and offered means: her passion, for its flight,
is tethered in the range of a command
and given opal wings whose insectine
fragility affords a fly's embrace
of sky. A heart she has, and yet her grace
and crystalline construction show no sign
of heart within, nor how they could contain
what she contains. Her madness, through its cage
of gilt, is rendered fine; aborted rage
bleeds quietly in pastel shades of pain.
And they are enchanted when she cries
with the exquisite greenness of her eyes.

SECRETOS DE FAMILIA

Mi cuñada oía voces
como Juana de Arco.

A veces estaban allí
mientras hablaban a larga distancia.
Querían matarla.
Le decías: oblígalo a dejar
el departamento, Jeannie. Bueno. Ya se ha ido.
Pero no estabas allí para el que
entró por la ventana mientras dormía,
con fotografías en su billetera del tiempo en que
ella lo amaba,
las plantas de sus pies endurecidas
por la arena del muelle de Santa Mónica.
Y llevaba algo más. La policía
no te quiso decir.
Bastante pesado como para quebrar un cráneo
a la carrera, antes de que los sueños
pudieran volver.

No era el Arcángel Miguel
a quien ella adoraba, después de todo, sino un hombre
con habilidad de asesino
en los músculos de sus manos.

Y padre.
Fotografías en la billetera. El verano
de camisas manchadas de césped y hermanos que vendían periódicos
y el padre, que mató a Princesa.
Trituró su cabeza con un martillo porque
la perra estaba en celo. Nadie
necesita esa sangre.
Y todos los meses después, con la nieve apilada

FAMILY SECRETS

My sister-in-law heard voices
like Joan of Arc.

Sometimes they would come
while you talked long distance.
They meant to kill her.
You would say: make him leave
the apartment, Jeannie. Okay. Now he's gone.
But you weren't there for the one
who climbed in a window while she slept,
with pictures in his wallet of when
she loved him,
their soles rubbed thick
by the sand on Santa Monica pier.
And he carried something else. The police
won't tell you what.
Heavy enough to break a skull
in a hurry, before the dreams
could be called back into it.

It wasn't the Archangel Michael
she was crazy about, it turns out, but a man
who carried the skill of murder
in the muscles of his hands.

And a father.
Pictures in her wallet. The summer
of grass-stained shirts and paperboy brothers
and the father, who killed Princess.
Crushed her head with a hammer because
the bitch went into heat. Nobody
needs that blood.
And all the months after, with snow piled deep

contra el taller cerrado,
los muchachos lanzaban restos de aluminio refulgente
como flechas en hombros blancos a la deriva
y nadie se preguntó qué es lo que hacía allí por tanto rato
con Jeannie, tanto rato.

Si ahora cierras tus ojos, ves a Jean
enamorada. Y a Princesa. Sangre en el césped,
hoyos rojos quemados por la nieve
dejando un camino hacia el taller,
hacia cualquier lugar,
hacia Santa Mónica.

Todos queremos que el funeral
sea más que esta caja con cenizas,
un sacerdote que besa su seda
como si fuera un banquete.
Tenemos hambre de confesión.
Los hombros del padre se levantan.
El bebé dentro de mí también se mueve,
recordándome de cómo la vida se convierte en una historia
que se contará un día.
La tía que alguien mató.

En esta estación, la familia pierde
y gana una.
Que rece el monseñor
para que descontemos nuestras pérdidas y quedemos a mano.

against the closed garage,
the boys threw aluminum flashing scraps
like spears into white drift shoulders
and nobody wondered what he was doing in there so long
with Jeannie, so long.

If you close your eyes now, picture Jean
in love. And Princess. Blood on the grass,
red holes burned in snow
leaving a trail to the garage,
to anywhere,
Santa Monica.

All of us want the funeral
to be more than this box of ash,
a priest who kisses his silk
like a good dinner.
We hunger for confession.
The father's shoulders heave.
The baby inside me also moves,
reminding me of how life becomes a story
to tell one day.
The aunt who someone killed.

This season, the family is losing
and gaining one.
Let the Monsignor pray
that we can cut our losses and call this even.

POR RICHARD DESPUES DE TODO

Por Richard después de todos
estos años, y por mí misma, soy

cuidadosa. Lectora paciente,
vigilante entre
piedras caídas:
                tu puedes, ¿sabías? escuchar
los labios del agua que se abren

y se cierran, observar

cómo caen al fondo, a velocidad de sueño,
identificarlas en descanso antes de dejar caer
la próxima. Así no es como me quedé
con él, una forma de vigilia en el café
nocturno, escuchando y no escuchando, inquieta
bajo las palabras y el tocadiscos automático que no iba
a ninguna parte, exactamente dos días antes

de que para sorpresa de todos menos para él
apareció muerto en el taller. Dejándome

con esa noche entera, limando márgenes
que no quieren suavizarse, ni siquiera
bajo una edad de hielo,
buscando la palabra que sucedió mientras yo
no escuchaba. Una piedra caída
en aguas profundas entre tantas otras piedras.

Richard me dejó con todos los otros amigos de mi vida:
para leerlos con cuidado, hasta el final, como
a libros prestados.

FOR RICHARD AFTER ALL

For Richard after all
these years, and for myself, I am

careful. A patient reader,
a waiter between
dropped stones:
                        you can, did you know? hear
the water's lips open

and close, watch it

fall to the bottom, dream-speed,
identify it at rest before dropping
the next one. This was not how I stayed

up with him, a kind of vigil in the all-night
coffee shop, listening and not listening, restless
under the words and the one-tune jukebox going
nowhere, exactly two days before

to the surprise of all but himself he was
dead in a garage. Leaving me

with that all-night, rubbing edges
that don't go smooth, not even
under an ice-age,
looking for the word that happened while I
didn't hear. A stone fallen in
deep water among so many other stones.

Richard left me with every other friend in my life:
to read them with care, to the end, like
borrowed books.

LA PERDIDA DE MIS BRAZOS Y PIERNAS

1.

El correo de ayer
me trajo, sin previo aviso,
la pérdida de mis brazos y piernas.
Leí la carta inmutable,
el hueso estalló
dentro de mi cráneo
y fluyó el aturdimiento,
como un glaciar,
por mi columna vertebral.
Se había detenido en el camino para ayudar a una mujer
con una llanta desinflada, mi amiga es generosa. El hombre
que la golpeó con su automóvil
nunca se detuvo.
Esta es la amiga a la que siempre
he visto calzada.
Ahora no puede enderezarse para verse los pies.
Esta noche me mantiene despierta el ladrido
de todos los perros en mi cerebro.
¿Es así como se siente?
Cuando todo lo que se tiene
queda enjaulado dentro de un cráneo,
porque puedes mirar el viento,
afuera, y ver
que hasta los árboles pueden moverse
pero tú
tienes que pedirle a alguien
que limpie y gire tu cuerpo
mientras esperas por todo el resto
de todo el tiempo
que te queda.

THE LOSS OF MY ARMS AND LEGS

1.

Yesterday's mail
brought me without warning
the loss of my arms and legs.
I read the permanent letter,
the bone snapped
under my skull
and numbness flowed
down my spine
like a glacier.
She had stopped to help a woman
with a flat, my friend is kind. The man
who hit her with his car
never stopped.
This is the friend I have always
known in shoes.
Now she can't sit up to see her feet.
Tonight I can't sleep for the barking
of all the dogs in my brain.
Is this how it is?
When everything you have
is boxed inside a skull,
because you can watch the wind
outside and see
that even trees can move
but you
have to ask someone
to wash and turn your body
while you wait out all the rest
of all the time
you will ever have.

2.

El monje budista,
con la cabeza contra el cielo, reza
para que se detengan las bombas.
Su piel es demasiado pura para haber caminado
junto a las autopistas:
desde Tokyo a Nagasaki.
Desde San Francisco hasta el desierto,
encrespado en llamas el ruedo amarillo
de sus túnicas. Siente, dice,
y yo siento el dolor de la mujer
que no pudo encontrar a su hermana.
Estoy frenética entre los escombros.
En las siluetas de los cuerpos
proyectados contra los ladrillos
en las murallas de los edificios
descubro sus pequeños huesos quemados.

3.

Yo soy el polvo que siente la bota.
He sentido el hambre hasta que se me ha caído el cabello
y me he comido las uñas.
He sido violada en Texas,
en Puerto Rico, en Mississippi
por un hombre blanco que usaba el odio
como un apodo amoroso; violada
en El Salvador, frente a Dios
y a la tumba que esperó
para acunarme; violada a punta de bayoneta

2.

The Buddhist monk,
with his head against the sky, prays
the bombs will stop.
His skin is too pure to have walked
beside highways:
from Tokyo to Nagasaki.
From San Francisco into the desert
with flames curling out of the yellow hems
of his robes. Feel, he says
and I feel the grief of the woman
who could not find her sister.
I am frantic in the rubble.
In the silhouettes of bodies
flashed against bricks
on the side of every building
I see her small, incinerated bones.

3.

I am the dirt that feels the boot.
I have starved until my hair fell out
and eaten my fingernails.
I have been raped in Texas,
Puerto Rico, Mississippi
by a white man who used hate
like a love name; raped
in Salvador, in front of God
and the grave that waited
to hold me; raped at bayonet point

en las montañas de Guatemala
mientras miraba los ojos redondos
de mis hijos, y oraba para que no sintieran nada,
y oraba para que sintieran para siempre.

4.

Me han dicho que no puedo permitir que las heridas
de todo el mundo sangren
en mi cuerpo:
que no quedará nada para mí.
Nada para amarrar las cintas
que los traigan a casa. Los hombres que arrojan bombas
y dejan a los pequeños despegándose la piel
de los brazos, sin entender.
Cintas de piel.
Tengo entendido que están ahorrando
sus lágrimas para sus hijas.

5.

Soy el único animal
que puede morir cien veces,
y aún sentir por dentro el miedo a la muerte.
Si esperamos supervivencia,
permítanme lo siguiente:
mientras me sigan abriendo heridas
déjenme sangrar.

in the mountains of Guatemala
while I looked into the round bird eyes
of my children, and prayed they were feeling nothing,
prayed they would feel forever.

4.

I'm told I cannot allow the wounds
of all the world to bleed
through my one body,
that I will have nothing left for my own.
Nothing for tying the ribbons
that bring them home. The men who drop bombs
that leave babies peeling the skin
from their arms in wonder.
Ribbons of it.
I understand they are saving
their tears for their daughters.

5.

I am the only animal
that can die a hundred times
and still fear death inside.
If we expect survival,
allow me this.
As long as I continue to be cut,
let me still bleed.

IV

THE BELIEVERS

LOS CREYENTES

somewhere in me too is the path
down to the creek gleaming in the dark, a
way out of there.

Sharon Olds

LOS PUENTES

a los músicos de Sabiá

Tus manos sobre la conga tienen plumas,
           un pájaro sin cuerpo
               suspendido
           entre dos alas.

Tus dedos enroscados sobre la kena
           son una enredadera vieja
       retoñando un temblor de hojas.

Tus voces son el único grito
               atrapado
           por años en mi pecho,
           un prisionero
       esperando el terremoto.

La guerra es el camino al fin
               de todo
           y de nada.

Los palos grandes son para los tambores, y los tambores,
               para bailar,
       y San Salvador es un suburbio
           de Los Angeles,
           y Managua
       uno de los barrios más ruidosos
           de Nueva York,
           y los puentes
           que tú construyes,
       ya están bajo mis pies.

BRIDGES

for the musicians of Sabiá

Your hands on the conga are feathered,
                        a bodiless bird
                        suspended
                between two wings.

Your fingers curled on the kena
                        are an old vine
                sprouting a shiver of leaves.

Your voices are the single cry
                        trapped
                in my breast for years,
                a prisoner
        waiting for the earthquake.

War is the means to the end
                        of everything
                and nothing.

Big sticks are for drums, and drums for
                        dancing
                and San Salvador is a suburb
                of Los Angeles,
                and Managua
        one of the noisier neighborhoods
                of Nueva York
                and the bridges
                you build
        are already under my feet.

PONIENDOME UN NOMBRE

He protegido mi nombre como la gente
de otras épocas guardaba mechones de su cabello,
creyendo que el alma podía fugarse
si no tenían cuidado.

Conocí a mi primer antepasado.
Su leyenda. He tocado
sus botas y el bigote, el abuelo
cuya familia era dueña de esclavos y algodón.
Se sentía inquieto en Virginia
entre sus hermanos aristócratas, hasta que
un otoño llameante robó un caballo,
y galopó sobre las montañas para desposar
a una cheroki de ojos en forma de hojas.
El robo fue perdonado, pero nunca
la sangre indígena. Perdió el nombre de familia
e inventó el mío, le dió frutos y semillas.
Nunca conocí a la abuela.
Su fotografía tiene delgadas trenzas color tinta
y ropas abotonadas, y ningún nombre por el cual se le conociera.

Podría deshacerme de mi nombre en la mitad de la vida,
la cosa más común, y desaparecería
junto con la niñez y las abuelas muertas
hacia ese limbo creado para los nombres de soltera fuera de circulación.

Pero se inquietaría allí.
Lo sé. Cabalgaría sobre montañas con humo de hojas
para robar caballos.

NAMING MYSELF

I have guarded my name as people
in other times kept their own clipped hair,
believing the soul could be scattered
if they were careless.

I knew my first ancestor.
His legend. I have touched
his boots and moustache, the grandfather
whose people owned slaves and cotton.
He was restless in Virginia
among the gentleman brothers, until
one peppered, flaming autumn he stole a horse,
rode over the mountains to marry
a leaf-eyed Cherokee.
The theft was forgiven but never
the Indian blood. He lost his family's name
and invented mine, gave it fruit and seeds.
I never knew the grandmother.
Her photograph has ink-thin braids
and buttoned clothes, and nothing that she was called.

I could shed my name in the middle of life,
the ordinary thing, and it would flee
along with childhood and dead grandmothers
to that Limbo for discontinued maiden names.

But it would grow restless there.
I know this. It would ride over leaf smoke mountains
and steal horses.

APOTEOSIS

Hay días en que tengo envidia de mis gallinas:
cuando siento hambre de un propósito tan perfecto y seguro
como un solo huevo diario.

Si sólo pudiera pararme al sol,
rascar la tierra y pestañear y esperar
a que los elementos dentro de mí se ensamblen,
pidiendo solamente granos, me rendiría ante el milagro
de la encarnación diaria: un día de mi alma
capturado en yema y cáscara.

Y no tendría necesidad
de las visiones que a otros les llegan
en alas de murciélagos, para llevarlos
cara a cara con la nada.
El aullido del coyote en la noche no erizaría mis plumas, porque yo,
adormecida en mi gallo, soñaría
con los frutos en réplica de mi vida
anidados y seguros en cajas de huevos.

Aún así, nunca me dejo seducir,
porque he visto lo que sabe una gallina de omnipotencia:
nada de los milagros de a docena,
sólo la mano que alimenta
y, diariamente, roba el nido.

APOTHEOSIS

There are days when I am envious of my hens:
when I hunger for a purpose as perfect and sure
as a single daily egg.

If I could only stand in the sun,
scratch the gravel and blink and wait
for the elements within me to assemble,
asking only grain I would
surrender myself to the miracle
of everyday incarnation: a day of my soul
captured in yolk and shell.

And I would have no need
for the visions that come to others
on bat's wings, to carry them
face to face with nothingness.
The howl of the coyote in the night
would not raise my feathers, for I,
drowsy on my roost, would dream
of the replicated fruits of my life
nested safe in cartons.

And yet I am never seduced,
for I have seen what a hen knows of omnipotence:
nothing of the miracles in twelves,
only of the hand that feeds
and, daily, robs the nest.

ORANG-OUTANG

Perseguidos
e inquietos en los desiertos, no concibieron ningún deseo.
Inferiores, cuadrúmanos,
no segaron una cosecha de preocupaciones
desde su oscuridad,
no podían saber
ni siquiera que los habíamos abandonado, para gobernar
y dominar,
ni que mediante algún principio del tiempo
también morimos
para vivir
y tener esperanzas de salvarnos de
estar perseguidos
e inquietos en el desierto donde no concebimos ningún deseo.

Las dos primeras líneas de este poema pertenecen al trabajo de Lamarck, *Philosophie Zoologique,*
"Transformación del orang-outang en la especie humana."

ORANG-OUTANG

Being persecuted
and restless in the deserts they conceived no wants.
Inferior, quadrumanous,
they reaped no burden harvest
from their darkness,
could not know
even that we had left them, come to rule
and hold dominion,
nor that through some principle of time
we die as well
that we might live
and hope to save ourselves from
being persecuted
and restless in the desert we conceive no wants.

The first two lines of this poem are taken from Lamarck's work *Philosophie Zoologique,*
"Transformation of the orang-outang into the human species."

UN SIMPLE MILAGRO

He llorado los días perdidos
cuando no logré nada de importancia.
Pero no últimamente.

Ultimamente, bajo la marea lunar
del océano de una mujer, busco
mi propio cambio en el mar:
transformar granos de arena en ojos humanos.
Sueño despierta después del desayuno
mientras el espíritu de huevos y tostadas
teje un largo de hueso
fino como espiga de trigo.
Más tarde, mientras aplazo desmalezar el jardín
haré dos manos
que cuiden cien jardines.

Necesito exactamente diez lunas llenas
para cumplir la promesa animal.
Me ofrezco, sin santidad, pero
transmutada de todas maneras
por el milagro más simple.
No soy nada en este mundo fuera de las cosas
que hace una mujer.
Pero aquí están los ojos que una vez fueron perlas.
Y aquí, un porvenir donde antes no hubo nada.

ORDINARY MIRACLE

I have mourned lost days
when I accomplished nothing of importance.
But not lately.

Lately, under the lunar tide
of a woman's ocean, I work
my own sea-change:
turning grains of sand to human eyes.
I daydream after breakfast
while the spirit of egg and toast
knits together a length of bone
as fine as wheatstalk.
Later, as I postpone weeding the garden
I will make two hands
that may tend a hundred gardens.

I need ten full moons exactly
for keeping the animal promise.
I offer myself up: unsaintly, but
transmuted anyway
by the most ordinary miracle.
I am nothing in this world beyond the things
one woman does.
But here are eyes that once were pearls.
And here is a second chance where there was none.

MELANCOLÍA INFANTIL

para Lily, al borde

Mírenme mi
oscuro corazón escarlata disfrazado de rosado
yo soy, ¡miren! ¡a! ¡mí!
Ay soy la pura fuerza azul de Querer
aullando a través de delgadas paredes
como un viento de pradera.
Soy tan grande y vacía.
¿Por qué los cereales se pegan al dorso de mis manos?
Cuando empujo al oso de la cuna,
¿por qué desaparece? Quiero ese oso.
Quiero
Ah escuchen, el estremecidocascabeleo de orejas levantándose
¡el perro! Ah venvenvenvenvenvenvenvenven
se fue.
Quiero ese perro.
Quédense con sus colores pastel.
El aburrimiento es una necesidad morada. El hambre es bermeja.
Quiero mi madremadre leche azul obscura celestial
pero en el minuto que caigo en la oscuridad ella me recuesta.
Lo hacen, te recuestan. Los grandes
solo quieren una cosa: dejarte sola.
Ves, tienes que quedarte despierta.
Los grandes son mi pastor y todo me faltará
por la pura fuerza azul
de un viento que aulla quiero
el perro el oso la leche quiero
cada cereal que cayó al suelo quiero
los colores más brillantes
pegados con fuerza contra mis encías
quiero
el mundo
y no cabe
en mi boca.

BABYBLUES

for Lily on the verge

Look at me my
dark scarlet heart disguised in pink
I am Look! At! Me!
Oh I'm the pure blue force of Want
howling through thin walls
like a prairie wind.
I am so large and empty.
Why do the cheerios stick to the backs of my hands?
When I push the bear through the bars,
why is it gone? I want that bear.
I want
Oh listen, the jingleshudder of ears getting up
the dog! Oh comecomecomecomecomecomecomecome
gone.
I want that dog.
Oh keep your pastel colors.
Boredom is a purple need. Hunger is vermilion.
I want my dark blue heaven milk mothermother
but the minute I fall into darkness she puts me down.
They do, they put you down. The big ones
only want one thing: to leave you alone.
You have to stay awake, see.
The big ones are my shepherd and I shall want
with the pure blue force
of a howling wind I want
the dog the bear the milk I want
every cheerio that fell on the floor I want
the brightest colors
all pressed hard against my gums
I want
the world
and it will not fit
in my mouth.

EL PAN DIARIO

para Steven

El tintineo de las tazas de medir en la cocina
despierta mis oídos. Cierro
el libro que estoy leyendo,
marco el lugar con el dedo
y escucho: a las tazas de medir,
pequeñas riñas de medio contra cuarto,
luego el acallado cernir de la harina.
Habrá amasado,
habrá aplacar lo fermentado,
y levantarse y levantarse otra vez,
la presión de aumento constreñido
por la pequeña caja cuadrada en el horno,
el inmutable paso del tiempo,
y finalmente un hogar y un cuerpo lleno
de oro fragante.
Vuelvo a mi libro, pero primero
agradezco a los dioses de la cocina
por lo que significa el matrimonio: por medio de este
inmutable pasaje, este imposible
constreñir cuadrado, estos tintineos triviales
de medio contra cuarto, y ay
este amasar, este aplacar para levantarse,
he sido bendecida
con un esposo que hace pan.

DAILY BREAD

for Steven

The clink of tin cups in the kitchen
rouses my ears. I close my book,
hold my place with a fingertip while
I listen: to the measuring cups,
little quarrels of half against quarter,
then the sifted hush of the flour.
There will be kneading,
there will be punching down,
and rising and rising again,
the press of increase constrained
by the small square box in the oven,
the immutable passage of time,
and finally a home and a hunger filled
with fragrant gold.
I return to my reading, but first
I thank the kitchen gods
for what marriage is: throughout this
immutable passage, these square
impossible constraints, these petty clinkings
of half against quarter, and oh
this needing, oh this falling and this rising,
I am blessed
with a husband who makes bread.

VERTIENTE

Afuera, los coyotes aúllan
como niños huérfanos, la luna
la única antigua fotografía de lata de su hogar.
En otras montañas como éstas, hay guerra.

Tus ojos nadan en brazadas rápidas
por cuevas mojadas y selladas, sus bocas
con tatuajes de sueños. Me pregunto
si estoy allí contigo,
si cuando tu aliento se desgrana en garras de acacia
y se libra, tú hablas alguna verdad
que nos pudiera salvar y que mañana
haya desaparecido perfectamente, un timbre dibujado en agua.

Tu sueño, y los coyotes
ya se aquietarán. El mundo podría acabarse
o empezar. Quedan dos horas para el amanecer.

Una vez el insomnio era el ladrón que odié,
el que se guardaba los triunfos de mañana en sus bolsillos.
Pero después de estos años me voy deshaciendo
de ambiciones triunfantes,
ese baño se ha puesto muy frío.

Puedo recostarme en la vertiente
de tu sueño, en cambio,
a mirar cómo los sueños pasan bajo
el perfecto acueducto de marfil de tus huesos.
Si hubiera dormido, habría sido sólo otra hora
en que te hubiera perdido para mí.

WATERSHED

Outside, coyotes wail
like orphaned children, the moon
their old tin photograph of home.
In other mountains like these, there is war.

Your eyes swim quick strokes
in sealed wet caves whose mouths
are tattooed with dreams. I wonder
if I'm there with you,
if, when your breath snags on acacia claws
and then pulls free, you are telling some truth
that could save us, that tomorrow will be
perfectly gone, a blueprint drawn on water.

Your sleep, and the coyotes
will quiet soon. The world might end
or begin. There are two good hours till dawn.

Insomnia was once the thief I hated,
tucking tomorrow's triumphs in his pockets.
But after these years I am easing myself out
of triumphant ambitions,
that bath has grown too cold.

I can lie here in the watershed
of your sleep, instead,
watching dreams pass under
the perfect ivory aquaduct of your bones.
Had I slept, it would only have been another hour
in which you were lost to me.

POSESION

Las cosas que deseo son:
un color. Un bosque.
El demonio y el hielo en mi boca.
Todo
lo que no se puede poseer.
Un leopardo, una vida, un beso.
Tú
nunca me defraudas.
El saber que también me has deseado
es tan bueno como el acto
de confiar.

POSSESSION

The things I wish for are:
A color. A forest.
The devil and ice in my mouth.
Everything
that can't be owned.
A leopard, a life, a kiss.
You
Never let me down.
To know that you have wanted me too
is as good as the deed
of trust.

CEMENTERIO DE FRANKFORT

para Steven

Era el tipo de lugar donde
los automóviles van a buscar la oscuridad.
Los sábados por la noche después de los juegos
y la larga espera.
Pasamos por alto las lápidas, ignoramos
el campo de huesos donde la muerte
desparrama largas raíces subterráneas,
levanta florescencias de piedra
que derraman un polen de nombres de familias
hacia un futuro infinito, con la esperanza de ser recibidos.
Nos sacudimos ese polen como abejas borrachas de primavera
que piensan vivir para siempre. Nos sacudimos
con la sola esperanza de ser recibidos.
Mi madre dijo que una dama sube los escalones uno a la vez,
pero subí volando con un muchacho de piel dulce
aprendiendo la lengua extranjera de palpar,
queriendo morir y renacer en un planeta
de seres que solamente se comunican
tocando labios contra piel: el Planeta Osculo.
Me mecí en una cuna de musgo erizado.
Tenía la mitad de mi edad.
Nada podía hacerme ver hasta
el lago de huesos a solo seis pies de hondo,
una superficie ondulante, a nivel, donde
la tiza perecedera de los padres
flotó como hombre muerto, y entre ellos
bebés, algunos, flotando,
levantándose con bocas abiertas hacia
los cumpleaños que tuvieron que sacrificar,
la exquisita atracción del tacto.

He querido atraerte de vuelta allí,
para conocerte en ese tiempo antes de conocerte,
y ofrecer el regalo del ciego primer amor.
Pero si ahora fuéramos allí, nuestro automóvil

FRANKFORT CEMETERY

for Steven

It was that kind of place where
cars go to be in the dark.
Saturday nights after games
and acute postponement,
we overlooked tombstones, ignored
the field of bones where death
spreads long roots underground,
pushes up stone inflorescences
that scatter a pollen of family names
to an infinite future, hoping to be received.
We shook off that pollen like spring-drunk bees
who plan on living forever. Shook
with the only hope of being received.
My mother said a lady walks up steps one at a time,
but I took whole flights with a sweet-skinned boy
learning the foreign tongue of touch,
wanting to die and be reborn on a planet
of beings who only communicate
by touching lips to skin: the Planet Oscula.
I rocked in a cradle of stickleback moss.
I was half as old as myself.
Nothing could make me see so far
as the lake of bones only six feet down,
a rippling, level surface where
the perishing chalk of the fathers
did a dead man's float, and among them even
babies—a few—treading water,
rising with open mouths toward
the birthdays they surrendered,
the exquisite pull of touch.

I have wanted to draw you back there,
to know you in that time before I knew you,
offer the gift of blind first love.
But if we went there now, our car

sería viejo, cómodo como un ataúd,
el asiento trasero un sombrío cojín de musgo.
Nos recostaríamos para exhalar,
hundirnos seis pies para flotar en ese lago de huesos
con todos los amores que hemos conocido y perdido,
los bebés perdidos, la tiza perecedera
de los padres. Podríamos ver en la oscuridad.
Y créeme: nada fue nunca mejor que esto, un amor
que hacemos con ojos abiertos entre nuestros muertos.
El aliento que tomamos de los pulmones del otro
para recobrar el descanso de una vida:
se revuelca entre nosotros como un pez,
arquea músculo contra nuestros estómagos. Nos abrazamos
fuerte, y flotamos en ese lago donde yo
me levanto a través tuyo hacia los cumpleaños
que nunca voy a ver,
la exquisita atracción del tacto,
me levanto a través tuyo. Me levanto
con la boca muy abierta.

would be old, comfortable as a coffin,
its back seat a somber cushion of moss.
We would lie down and exhale,
sink down six feet to float on that lake of bones
with all the loves we have known and lost,
the babies lost, the perishing chalk
of the fathers. We would see in the dark.
And believe me: nothing was ever
better than this, a love
we make wide-eyed among our dead.
The breath we take from each other's lungs
to recover the rest of a life:
it thrashes between us like a fish,
arches muscle against our bellies. We hold
tight, and float on that lake where I
rise up through you toward the birthdays
I will never see,
the exquisite pull of touch,
I rise up through you. Rise up
with my mouth wide open.

POEMA PARA UNA VECINA MUERTA

Yo amarraba enredaderas de tomates,
oculta hasta los codos y cegada por lágrimas
de olor de ortiga
el día en que te encontraron muerta.

Sé que amabas mi jardín
más que a los familiares que no te visitaban.
Como ellos, estaba vivo y cambiaba
un poquito cada día
exactamente como lo esperabas.
Me observabas por sobre la reja
como mira una madre
separada de sus hijos.
Por la noche descorrías el cerrojo
con manos huesudas, y te deslizabas
a regar y sacar las hojas secas
de mi negligencia.

Hacías ruido de flema en tu gran casa
vacía ahora por la partida de tu dulce esposo,
como le llamabas. El había venido primero
por las llanuras para esperarte:
su novia de la frontera de Missouri,
que se hizo joven en un pueblo de tierra y herraduras,
con una casa que ordenar,

POEM FOR A DEAD NEIGHBOR

I was tying up tomato vines,
elbow-deep and blinded by tears
in their nettle smell
on the day they found you dead.

I know you loved my garden
instead of kin who didn't visit.
Like them, it was alive and daily
a little changed
exactly as you expected.
You watched me over the fence
the way a mother
barred from her own children
watches.
At night you unlatched the gate
with knucklebone hands, and stole in
to water and pick brown leaves
when I was negligent.

You rattled like phlegm in your big house
left empty by the departure
of your sweet husband,
as you called him. He had come first
over the plains, and waited for you:
his frontier bride from Missouri,
teenaged in a town of dirt and horseshoes,
with a house to keep,

una tormenta de hojas secas en tus ventanas
que nadie sino tú recuerda,
son tu jardín.

Cuando me regalaste tu vestido de novia
para salvarlo de consumirse
en tu casa agonizante,
lo tomé, pero no lo quería.
Terciopelo negro.
¿Cómo podía ser el amor el color de la muerte,
la tela del silencio de la noche?
Reímos, pero corrimos como caballos asustados
para ver que me quedaba perfectamente.

En tu funeral voy a ser una de más
en la docena de hijas con la conciencia sucia
y sus esposos de cuello y corbata.
Pensaré en tu casa de resuellos,
tosiendo por fin sus ruidos
hacia el silencio,
pero te dejaré allí
en la cómoda de mármol
que contiene a tu dulce esposo.
El no ha hecho nada más que esperar a su novia.

Y cuando no pueda dormir me pondré el vestido
de tu noche de silencio,
y me deslizaré hacia mi propio jardín.

a storm of brown leaves at your windows
that no one remembers but you,
they are your garden.

When you gave me your wedding dress,
to save it from the consumption
in your dying house, I
took it, but didn't want it.
Black velvet.
How could love be the color of death,
the cloth of a silent night?
We laughed, but shifted like spooked horses
to see that it fit me perfectly.

At your funeral I will make the baker's dozen
among the guilty daughters
and neck-tied husbands.
I'll think of your wheezing house,
the last rattle finally
coughed out of it,
but leave you there
in the marble chest of drawers
containing your sweet husband.
He has done nothing there but wait for his bride.

And when I can't sleep I'll wear the dress
of your silent night,
and steal into my own garden.

V

THE PATRIOTS

LOS PATRIOTAS

*It is either the beginning or the end
of the world, and the choice is ourselves
or nothing.*

                        Carolyn Forché

PADRE NUESTRO QUE AHOGAS
A LOS PAJAROS

en memoria de los nicaragüenses asesinados por los contras, 1980–1990.

Hay una época en que terminan las guerras:
es la estación de las lluvias.
Cuando el paisaje abre sus ojos
y se ríe de tu hablar de muerte.
Cuando todos los árboles muertos
abren sus manos
al cielo
y desde las puntas de sus dedos
sangran flores escarlata,
y es entonces que recuerdas que, antes de la sangre,
el color que te gustaba era el rojo.

Hay una época cuando toda cólera milenaria
se sosiega, concediendo
el agua a la hierba.
Cuando se resquebrajan las noches con las brillantes
voces eléctricas de tus antepasados,
y los que eran dueños de tus antepasados
llamándose unos a otros
entre tierra y cielo;
y todos los viejos rencores
se derrumban, uno a uno,
sobre el techo de tu casa
arrullando, cadenciosos,
el sueño de tus hijos.

Esta es la estación que iguala
todas las cosas,
la estación del Creador–incendiario.
Cuando el sol enciende un fuego en las nubes
y no se puede distinguir de la mañana.
Cuando ocaso y fuego y amanecer

OUR FATHER WHO DROWNS THE BIRDS

in memory of Nicaraguans killed by the Contras, 1980–1990.

There is a season when all wars end:
when the rains come.
When the landscape opens its own eyes
and laughs at your talk of dying.
When all the dead trees
open their hands
to the sky
and bleed scarlet flowers
from their fingertips,
and then you remember, before the blood,
red was the color you loved.

There is a season when every ancient anger
settles, conceding
to water the grass.
When nights are split by the bright
electric voices of your ancestors,
and the ones who owned your ancestors,
calling to one another
between earth and sky,
and all of the old grudges
fall, one by one,
on the roof of your house
sounding so much alike
they lull your babies to sleep.

This is the season that renders
all things equal:
the season of the arsonist-Creator.
When sun sets a fire in the clouds
that is indistinguishable from morning.
When sunset and fire and morning

todas son la misma palabra. Cuando mujer y hombre
son la misma palabra. Cuando justicia
no es una palabra
porque es aire, y lo respiramos.

Aún los animales recordarán esta estación:
aquellos que maldicen,
y aquellos que danzan porque
bajo la lluvia son iguales.
Los más tímidos se arrastran
desde sus hogares secretos y húmedos
para reunirse con sus hermanos de piel dura,
lejos de la sombra del carnívoro.
Hoy no hay sombras.
Las criaturas perseguidas
están encubiertas de lluvia, invisibles
y despojadas de miedo.

Y los cazadores,
las aves de rapiña de Norte América,
aventurándose demasiado lejos de su territorio,
cada uno atareándose bajo su única,
lenta, batiente ala:
los cazadores se cansan.
Aún las leyes naturales que los impulsan
son extranjeras en estos montes
de la otra América
cuando las lluvias llegan, por fin.
Sus bocas de rapiña se sofocan
de nubes, se ahogan en el aire mojado.
Desde tu distancia,

are all the same word. When woman and man
are the same word. When justice
is not a word
because it is air, and we breathe it.

Even the animals will remember this season:
those that curse,
and those that dance because
in the rain they are equal.
The timid ones
creep from their secret wet homes
to move with their thicker-skinned brothers,
move from the predator's shadow.
Today there are no shadows.
The hunted creatures
are cloaked in rain, invisible
and fearless.

The hunters,
North American birds of prey
foraging too far from their own territory,
each laboring under its one
slow, beating wing:
the hunters grow heavy.
Even the natural laws that propel them
are foreign in these hills
of the other America
when the rains come, finally.
Their raven mouths suffocate
in clouds, drown in wet air.
From your distance
you see the horizon shimmer where they fall,

ves resplandecer el horizonte donde
una a una, caen sobre los montes.
Una gran flor anaranjada incandescente
se levanta suavemente de cada tumba.
Esta es la estación en que terminan las guerras.

Y después, cuando los hijos de tus
hijos te pregunten por este día,
les dirás:
  En el octavo día hizo Dios justicia.
  En el octavo día envió Dios las lluvias
  a la otra América,
  para ahogar a los pájaros, y darnos una oportunidad de lucha.
Y los pequeños te creerán porque
en aquellos días los niños crecerán
con sus corazones intactos.

one by one, in the hills.
A great orange flower of heat
rises quietly from each grave.
This is the season when all wars end.

And after, when the children of your
children ask you about this day,
you will tell them:
    On the eighth day God made justice.
    On the eighth day God sent the rains
    to the other America,
    to drown the birds, and give us a fighting chance.
And the little ones will believe you because
in those days children will grow
with their hearts intact.

LA MAÑANA EN QUE DESCUBRI
QUE MI TELEFONO ESTABA INTERVENIDO

La mañana en que descubrí que mi teléfono estaba intervenido
me senté tras todos los cerrojos de mi casa
e hice memoria de lo que había sido robado,
recordé la vez en que vi el estómago de un animal
abierto frente a mí.

Si no tiene nada que esconder,
dicen ellos.

Conté todas las veces que en un mes
había tocado mi boca:
para hablar con mi madre, mi hermana,
el doctor que conoce mi útero,
una amiga con cáncer,
el hombre cuyas manos
me tocan cuando duermo.

Si no tiene nada que esconder,
dicen ellos,
vendrá un hombre con identificación especial.

Es increíble cómo las cosas simples pueden ser transformadas.
Me han dicho que agentes de mi país
entrenan a agentes de otros países—principalmente
pequeños y lejanos—en el uso del teléfono:
dos alambres se cortan y se adhieren,
uno a la lengua,
uno a los genitales.
Este es un efectivo método para enterarse de secretos.

Si no tiene nada que esconder,
dicen ellos,

ON THE MORNING I DISCOVERED
MY PHONE WAS TAPPED

On the morning I discovered my phone was tapped
I sat behind all the locks in my house
and remembered what was stolen,
remembered the time I saw an animal's belly
slit open in front of me.

If you have nothing to hide,
they say.

I counted every time in a month
it had touched my mouth:
to talk to my mother, my sister,
the doctor who knows my uterus,
a friend with cancer,
the man whose hands
touch me when I sleep.

If you have nothing to hide,
they say,
then a man with a special badge will come

The simplest things have uses beyond conception.
I am told that agents of my country
train agents of other countries—mainly small
and far away—in the use of the telephone:
two of the wires are cut and attached
one to the tongue,
one to the genitalia.
This is an effective way of learning secrets.

If you have nothing to hide,
they say,

vendrá un hombre con identificación especial
a su casa, y observará cómo se desviste.

Si voy a vivir en una casa donde incluso mi cráneo
tiene ventanas, y se investigan
las partes blandas de mi cerebro en busca de posibles crímenes,
prefiero entregar mis secretos
antes de que me los roben:

Primero, no soy fastidiosa.
Por las noches, mi casa es gobernada
por escarabajos duros de color café
que se arrastran desde las grietas mojadas de las cañerías.
Si mi patio tuviera ratas las invitaría a entrar.
De esto estoy segura. He dejado comida
sin tocar por días,
por haber visto una foto de ojos hambrientos en el periódico.

Segundo, a veces tengo terror de cosas ridículas,
especialmente en la noche,
sin embargo cuando duermo estoy desnuda.
Envuelta en fiebre de frazadas
hablo con las caras del periódico,
me apuro para alcanzarlos en las piedras
de los caminos de pequeños y lejanos países.
En mis manos repletas
ofrezco las monedas de mi nacimiento
a cambio de las de ellos, como si éstas
tuvieran el mismo valor.

Tercero, no me arrepiento.

Entre 1983 y 1985, el FBI investigó a miembros de más de 300 organizaciones de derechos
humanos en los Estados Unidos, alegando conexiones con el terrorismo internacional. En
1988, el FBI admitió que la investigación no tenía fundamento.

then a man with a special badge will come
to your house, and watch you undress.

If I am to live in a house where even my skull
has windows, and men probe
the soft parts of my brain for potential crimes,
I would rather give my secrets
than have them stolen:

First, I am not fastidious.
My house is ruled at night
by hard brown beetles
that crawl from wet crevices in the plumbing.
If my yard had mice I would ask them in.
I know this. I have left food
uneaten for days,
because of hungry eyes in a newsprint photograph.

Second, I am sometimes terrified of ridiculous things,
especially at night,
and yet I am naked when I sleep.
Wrapped in a fever of sheets
I talk to the newsprint faces,
hurry to catch up to them over stones
in the roads of small and distant countries.
In clutched handfuls
I hold out the coins of my birth
in exchange for theirs, as if these currencies
were of equal value.

Third, I am not repentant.

Between 1983 and 1985, the FBI investigated members of more than 300 human rights or-
ganizations in the U.S., alleging links with international terrorism. In 1988, the Bureau ad-
mitted the investigation was groundless.

LA HIJA SEGUNDA

Si la lanzaras al agua
flotaría río arriba.
¿Qué si el niño Moisés hubiera flotado río arriba,
meciéndose hacia el Lago Victoria
en su pequeña embarcación de juncos,
pasando frente a las transfiguradas lavanderas
dejándolas atrás en sorprendida vigilia?
¿Qué habría sido entonces de los hijos de Israel?
Esta hija segunda olvida
que existe la historia.

Si le muestras blanco, ella ve negro.
Tiene problemas con su vista.
Desde la infancia ha lanzado lejos
todos los colores en que la envolvimos:
primero el rosado, desdeñosa,
y luego también el azul, por razones por las
que no nos atrevimos a dar las gracias.
Ella dice que quiere ponerse rojo o nada.
Y debieras verla con su blusa roja
batiéndose contra su pequeño cuerpo delgado
como un solo de bandera,
marchando con el río,
guiando al salmón a la masacre.
Ella dice que en realidad no están muriendo.
Dice que algo te nace al nadar río arriba,
algo que busca su camino de vuelta al mar
y se propaga como hierba incendiada por entre las algas
a través del suelo de continentes sumergidos
y finalmente vuelve al mismo río,
no sólo uno, sino miles de peces,
una generación de peces.
Esta hija segunda cree que
ella quedará en la historia.

THE MIDDLE DAUGHTER

If you threw her in the water
she would float upstream.
What if baby Moses had floated upstream,
bobbing toward Lake Victoria in his bullrush boat,
passing the transfixed laundry women,
leaving them behind in a wake of amazement?
What would have become of the children of Israel?
This middle daughter forgets,
there is always history.

Show her white, she sees black.
The problem is her vision.
From infancy she has thrown off
every color we wrapped her in:
first the pink, contemptuous,
and later even the blue, for reasons
we hadn't the nerve to be thankful for.
She wants to wear red, or nothing.
And you should see her with her red shirt
flapping on her spindle body
like some solo flag,
marching up the river,
leading the salmon to slaughter.
She says they aren't really dying.
She says something is born of swimming upstream
that finds its way back to the sea
and spreads like a grassfire through the seaweed
across the floor of underwater continents
and finally comes back to the very same river,
not one, but a thousand fish,
a generation of fish.
This middle daughter believes
she will make history.

EN LA CIUDAD RODEADA DE GIGANTES

Cuando Dios era un niño
y el vampiro huía
ante el signo de la cruz,
era posible la fe.
Así de simple era la supervivencia.
Pero el salvador que la mano apretaba en el bolsillo
dio ánimo a los vampiros a prosperar en el bosque.

El error
fue llevar la cruz,
la patita de conejo,
San Cristóbal que protege
contra los accidentes:
robar coliflores
proliferando en jardines de chatarra.
Y por último, creer en los refugios atómicos.

Ahora nos han abandonado en ciudades rodeadas de gigantes.

Los Titanes, en sus hondas madrigueras secretas,
rodearon mi ciudad durante media vida
esperando su comparendo
o un fósforo encendido que tocara
el primero de ellos como una mecha, una guirnalda
de llamas líquidas para rodear a los muertos coronados.

Somos los hijos despojados de talismanes
que nos protejan en contra de la promesa
de aquellos que frotan la lámpara maravillosa
y conjuran el fuego. Conjuran
la oscuridad en la luz.
Somos los hijos criados para temer a Dios,

IN THE CITY RINGED WITH GIANTS

When God was a child
and the vampire fled
from the sign of the cross,
belief was possible.
Survival was this simple.
But the saviour clutched in the pocket
encouraged vampires to prosper in the forest.

The mistake
was to carry the cross,
the rabbit's foot,
St. Christopher who presides
over the wrecks,
steel cauliflowers
proliferating in junkyard gardens.
And finally, to believe in the fallout shelter.

Now we are left in cities ringed with giants.

The Titans in their secret slingshot burrows
encircled my city for half a lifetime
waiting for their subpoena,
or for a match to strike, touch
the first like a fuse, a crown
of liquid flame surrounding us, the coronated dead.

We are the children bereft of talismans
to hold against the promise
of those who would rub the lantern
and conjure fire. Conjure
darkness out of light.
We are bred to be God-fearing,

para extender nuestras manos asustadas
a la lámpara maravillosa que nos protegerá un día.

Somos los hijos herejes
que cometen todos los errores
menos éste:
no creemos en la lámpara.
Si se nos da bastante tiempo
derrocharemos nuestra herencia de holocausto
en las pequeñas monedas de las fogatas
y las velas en los pasillos.
Podemos ver más allá del fantasma
con figura de hongo,
hacia más allá de las montañas, un simple verdor de árboles.

Se nos llama ciegos.
Y nos movemos como blancos peces hacia la luz,
por el sendero
de nuestro propio instinto,
para vivir como si nuestras vidas nos pertenecieran.
En el suelo del bosque
danzaremos en un círculo de hongos encantados,
pisoteando el centro de las raíces,
danzando hasta que Dios
haya encontrado su segunda
niñez, y así es como sobreviviremos a los gigantes.

to stretch our frightened hands
to the magic lamp that someday will protect us.

We are the heretic children
who make all mistakes but this one:
we don't believe in the lantern.
Given time enough, we will
squander our inheritance of holocaust
in the small change of bonfires
and candles in the passageways.
We see beyond the phantasm
of mushroom shapes
to the mountains beyond. A simple green of trees.

We are the so-called blind.
And so we move
like white cave fish toward light,
along the path
of our only instinct,
to live as if our lives belonged to us.
On the forest floor
we dance in the fairy ring,
trample the root-cloth center
that sustains the mushroom circle,
dance until God
has found his second
childhood, and we have outlived the giants.

LA SANGRE REGRESA

1.

Los perros que merodean nuestras casas
son descendientes de lobos.
Dicen que la sangre regresa, que si
los dejáramos, nuestros regalones correrían hambrientos
por los bosques,
se harían señas unos a otros
con sus ojos y sus colas,
para ir de caza
escuchando a sus ancianos como antes.

2.

El hombre que no puede perdonarse a sí mismo
todavía usa el cabello de corte cuadrado.
Ha hecho una carrera de líneas más derechas
que su corte. Lo obligaron
a caminar entre muchedumbres
de puños tan apretados como esposas enterradas,
de gritos, las únicas dos palabras
de su lenguaje que conocían:
G-I-Joe y Sonofabitch.
Le pasaron una serpiente de soga blanca
por la espalda, subiendo
desde las muñecas,
apretando los brazos jóvenes
hasta los codos, luego hasta sus hombros,
donde el dolor
empujó su memoria contra
la lista del regimiento:

THE BLOOD RETURNS

1.

The dogs that slink through our houses
are descended from wolves.
They say the blood returns, that if
we let them, our pets would run hungry
through the forests,
signal to each other
with their eyes and tails,
for the hunt,
listen to their elders in the old way.

2.

The man who can't forgive himself
still wears his hair cut square.
He has made a career of straighter
lines than this. They made him
walk in crowds
of fists as tight as buried wives,
of shouts, the only two words
of his language they knew:
G-I-Joe and *Sonofabitch*.
They threaded behind his back
a slim white boa of rope that climbed
from the wrists,
constricted his sapling arms
to the elbows, then the shoulders,
where pain pushed his memory flat
against the boot-camp list:

porque soy más hombre que Charlie Cong.
Dice que le asombró descubrir
que su lista no era lo bastante larga.
Recordó a su esposa, sus muñecas
como finas cópulas de bronce bajo el terciopelo,
lejos como un sueño de este lugar, el único
hogar que necesitaba protección.
Confesó los nombres de las aldeas
programadas para el bombardeo.

3.

Afuera, cerca de un árbol de flores blancas,
la voz de la mujer canta
en mis oídos extranjeros, aunque las palabras
no son música. Me cuenta
cómo le metían agujas
bajo las uñas.
Despliega sus manos de azafrán,
mostrando donde los pétalos fueron
arrancados desde la base. Dice
que sólo pensaba en sus hijos,
escuchaba sus nombres en el lenguaje uniforme
de sus preguntas. Hicieron
otras cosas, dice,

Why I am more of a man than Charlie Cong.
He says he was amazed to find
the list not long enough.
He imagined his wife, her wrists
like fine brass couplings under velvet,
dream-miles from this place, the only
home in need of protection.
He gave up the names of villages
scheduled for bombing.

3.

Outside, near a white tree of flowers,
the woman's voice sings
in my foreign ears, though the words
are not music. She is
telling me how they pushed needles
under her fingernails.
She spreads her crocus hands,
shows me where the petals tore
from the base. She thought of nothing
but her children,
heard their names in the uniform language
of their questions. They did
other things, she says,

protegiendo sus pezones
y le pregunto si confesó.
Ella se inclina hacia mis delgados párpados
como si yo fuera muy pequeña.
"He dado a luz el dolor con cada uno de mis pequeños.
¿Cómo podría el dolor hacer a una madre
entregar a sus hijos?"

4.

En el campamento verde oliva
en los pinos secretos de Georgia,
se entrenan a hombres para que regresen
a su país, en el sur,
como soldados extranjeros.
Para trabajar en grupos de seis:
para mutilar un cuerpo de seis formas,
todas mortales,
para que la culpa se diluya
como el vino malo se corta con el agua.
Pero el corazón es una cámara que se vuelve a llenar
ante la vista de las aldeas de rojo barro
y mujeres cocinando tortillas.
La sangre regresa. Los soldados están desertando.
Su estudio de la guerra era un arado de intrigas y vidrio
y el hogar es la tierra animal que no cede.
La única lucha se encuentra aquí.

shielding her nipples
and I ask her if she spoke.
She leans over my thin eyelids
as if I were very young.
"I have borne pain with each one of my babies.
How could pain make a mother
give back her children?"

4.

In the olive green camp
in the secret pines of Georgia
men are trained to return to their own
country, to the south,
as foreign soldiers.
To work in teams of six:
mutilate a body in six ways,
each one deadly,
so guilt is diluted
like bad wine cut with water.
But the heart is a chamber that fills again
at the sight of red mud villages,
women pounding tortillas.
The blood returns. The soldiers are deserting.
Their study of war was a plowshare of schemes and glass
and home is the unyielding animal soil.
The only fight is here.

RECUERDA: LA LUNA SOBREVIVE

A Pamela

Recuerda: la luna sobrevive,
se levanta delgada-creciente,
una mujer en curva. Intocable,
se inclina alrededor de la sombra
que se aprieta contra ella, y

espera. Recuerda cómo esperaste
cuando las noches sangraron su obscuridad
como tinta, para ennegrecer los días de más allá,
para enceguecer el único ojo de la mañana.
Así es como aprendiste a dibujar
tu vida como la luna,
enroscada como un feto alrededor de

la sombra. Enroscada en tu cama,
las pequeñas flores esperanzadas de tus rodillas
apretadas contra la pared,
su remedo de pintura,
siempre los colores de niña pequeña
sobre las piedras de la prisión común:
la casa donde eras hija de alguien,
hermana, carne de alguien, sangre

de alguien. El Cordero y María
te han dejado flotando en esta obscuridad
como un hueso de sopa. Observas
la fiesta de caníbales desde un escondrijo
y oras para deshacerte de tu ofrenda.
Todo lo que quieres es el sol,

REMEMBER THE MOON SURVIVES

for Pamela

Remember the moon survives,
draws herself out crescent-thin,
a curved woman. Untouchable,
she bends around the shadow
that pushes himself against her, and she

waits. Remember how you waited
when the nights bled their darkness out
like ink, to blacken the days beyond,
to blind morning's one eye.
This is how you learned to draw
your life out like the moon,
curled like a fetus around the

shadow. Curled in your bed,
the little hopeful flowers of your knees
pressed against the wall,
its mockery of paint,
always the little-girl colors
on the stones of the ordinary prison:
the house where you are someone's
daughter, sister, someone's flesh, someone's

blood. The Lamb and Mary
have left you to float in this darkness
like a soup bone. You watch
the cannibal feast from a hidden place
and pray to be rid of your offering.
The sun is all you wait for,

la luz, santo protector de todos los niños
que duermen como la muerte en el despertar

del crimen familiar. Detienes
tu corazón como un reloj: estas horas
no son tuyas. Ocultas
tu vida, escondes rápida la moneda de la suerte
en tu zapato
para cuando venga

el ladrón. Porque vendrá,
tan seguro como tus zapatos. Este es el que posee
todas las llaves de tu vivienda,
al que no puedes escapar, y mientras
tu corazón se detiene, te roba.
Te llevará años

aprender: por qué negaste el sueño
a la boca que se abría en la sombra;
por qué no la alimentabas con
los sueños que guardaste con hermetismo
en una caverna de lágrimas; por qué
todavía te visita la viuda negra,
exprimiendo su veneno gota a gota,
en una sarta granate
sobre tu abdomen,

the light, guardian saint of all the children
who lie like death on the wake

of the household crime. You stop
your heart like a clock: these hours
are not your own. You hide
your life away, the lucky coin
tucked quickly in the shoe
from the burglar, when he

comes. Because he will, as sure
as shoes. This is the one
with all the keys to where you live,
the one you can't escape, and while
your heart is stopped, he takes things.
It will take you years

to learn: why you held back sleep
from the mouth that opened in the dark;
why you would not feed it with
the dreams you sealed up tight
in a cave of tears; why
the black widow still visits you,
squeezes her venom out in droplets,
stringing them like garnets
down your abdomen,

las joyas de terror de una mujer
que llevabas adentro, una niña pequeña
a quién robaron

en la obscuridad. Finalmente lo sabes.
Has abierto tu aturdimiento en rebanadas
con los cuchillos de tus propios ojos.
De tantos años de observar
te han crecido pupilas de gato, para ver

en la obscuridad. Y estos ojos son
tu bendición. Siempre conocerán el veneno
de las joyas incrustadas
en tu carne.
Siempre conocerán la obscuridad
que ahora ya es uno de tus nombres,
pero no el nombre al que respondes.
Tú eres la que sabe que, detrás del
ascenso y la caída de la marea
de sombra, la luna siempre

está entera. Tus ojos acogen
el plateado y lo clavas ajustándolo
como poemas en acero
en la fina, brillante creciente de tu vida:
la hoz,
el feto,
la luna, que sobrevive.

the terrifying jewelry of a woman
you wore inside, a child robbed

in the dark. Finally you know this.
You have sliced your numbness open
with the blades of your own eyes.
From your years of watching
you have grown the pupils of a cat, to see

in the dark. And these eyes are
your blessing. They will always know the poison
from the jewels that are both embedded
in your flesh.
They will always know the darkness
that is one of your names by now,
but not the one you answer to.
You are the one who knows, behind
the rising, falling tide
of shadow, the moon is always

whole. You take in silver
through your eyes, and hammer it
as taut as poems in steel
into the fine bright crescent of your life:
the sickle,
the fetus,
the surviving moon.

LOS OJOS DE TU MADRE

a Maura y Lesbia López

Maura, tu vida ha estado en mis sueños:
allí hay lirios rojos como sangre, como amanecer,
que sólo se levantan desde las cicatrices
que deja en la tierra un gran fuego.

Maura, tu madre tenía dieciséis años, aún no te pensaba,
cuando la sorprendieron pintando paredes,
pintando el más antiguo de los mañanas
con colores que encontró tan sólo dentro de sus propios ojos.
Cuando tu madre tenía dieciséis, esto era una acción criminal.

Maura, ella nunca te dirá todo
lo que sucedió en la prisión: aquellos hombres
de pantalones metidos en las botas, el dolor.
Cómo lo observó arreglarse la camisa,
preguntándose si sería posible
volver a encontrar un motivo de amor.
Muy poco después empezó a pensar en ti.

Maura, hubo gente que dijo que no deberías
venir al mundo, que una vida concebida en odio
será más odio que vida. Tu madre dijo
que la semilla es lo más pequeño de un árbol
que ha vivido muchas estaciones.
Aún antes de convertirse en capullo, la semilla
ya no es lo que fue. Así fue como naciste
y en la estación que te dio a luz
doblaron todas las campanas del país,
prometiendo generosidad, el más antiguo
de los mañanas.
Hasta los hombres de las botas fueron tratados con generosidad.

Maura, tienes los ojos de tu madre.

YOUR MOTHER'S EYES

for Maura and Lesbia Lopez

Maura, I have dreamed of your life:
there are lilies as red as blood, as a sunrise
that only grow from scarred earth after a fire.

Maura, your mother was sixteen, without thoughts of you,
when they caught her painting walls,
painting the oldest kind of tomorrow
in colors she found only inside her eyes.
When your mother was sixteen, this was a crime.

Maura, she will never tell you everything
they did to her in prison: the men,
the pants tucked into boots, the pain.
The way she watched him tuck his shirttail in
while she wondered what she would ever
find to love again.
Soon after this, she began to think of you.

Maura, there were people who said you should not
be born, that a life conceived in hatred
is more hate than life. Your mother said
the seed is the least of a tree
that has lived through several seasons.
Even before the first bud opens, the seed
is not what it was. And so you were born
and in the season that brought you into the light
they rang every bell in the country, down to the sea
and promised kindness, the oldest
kind of tomorrow.
Even the men in boots were treated with kindness.

Maura, you have your mother's eyes.

Selected Titles from Seal Press

NOWLE'S PASSING by Edith Forbes. $12.00, 1-878067-99-0. A beautifully crafted novel about a woman who faces her exacting family legacy to discover her own life.

NERVOUS CONDITIONS by Tsitsi Dangarembga. $12.00, 1-878067-77-X. A lyrical story of a Zimbabwean girl's coming-of-age and a compelling narrative of the devastating human loss involved in the colonization of one culture by another.

WHERE THE OCEANS MEET by Bhargavi C. Mandava. $12.00, 1-58005-000-X. This incantatory debut novel explores the rich textures of Indian culture through the lives of four Indian and Indian-American women.

IF YOU HAD A FAMILY by Barbara Wilson. $12.00, 1-878067-82-6. An unforgettable novel about a woman who struggles to come to terms with memories of her childhood and finds a greater understanding of what family is and can be.

WORKING PARTS by Lucy Jane Bledsoe. $12.00, 1-878067-94-X. This first novel explores the essence of friendship and the potential unleashed when we face our most intense fears.

AN OPEN WEAVE by devorah major. $20.95, 1-878067-66-4 (cloth). This strong debut novel creates a rich portrait of three generations of an African-American family.

LOVERS' CHOICE by Becky Birtha. $10.95, 1-878067-41-9. An evocative collection of stories charting the course of black women's lives.

DISAPPEARING MOON CAFE by Sky Lee. $10.95, 1-878067-12-5. A spellbinding first novel that portrays four generations of the Wong family in Vancouver's Chinatown.

WORDS OF FAREWELL: STORIES BY KOREAN WOMEN WRITERS by Kang Sok-kyong, Kim Chi-won and O Chong-hui. $12.00, 0-931188-76-8. Short stories by three highly regarded Korean women writers. Winner of the Korean Translation Prize.

ANGEL by Merle Collins. $9.95, 0-931188-64-4. This vibrant novel from Grenada follows young Angel McAllister as she joins her country's move toward political autonomy.

EGALIA'S DAUGHTERS by Gerd Brantenberg. $12.95, 1-878067-58-3. A hilarious satire on sex roles by Norway's leading feminist writer.

LATIN SATINS by Terri de la Peña. $10.95, 1-878067-52-4. Full of humor and tenderness, this novel tells the story of the lives and loves of a group of young Chicana lesbian singers.

Seal Press publishes fiction, poetry and non-fiction books by women authors. You may order directly from us at 3131 Western Avenue, Suite 410, Seattle, WA 98121 (add 16.5% of the total book order for shipping and handling; Washington residents must pay 8.6% sales tax). Write to us for a free catalog or visit our website at <www.sealpress.com>.